Science Skills

6

Pupil's Book

by

Jocelyne Churchill

CAMBRIDGE
UNIVERSITY PRESS

SCIENCE SKILLS 6

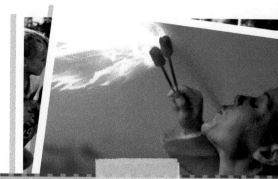

Contents

1 Interaction
- Sense organs
- Nervous system
- Musculoskeletal system
- Reflexes

2 Nutrition
- Stages of nutrition
- Food groups and nutrients
- Digestive system
- Circulatory system
- Respiratory and excretory systems
- First-aid techniques

3 We are nature
- Five kingdoms
- Photosynthesis
- Water, a limited resource
- Caring for living things
- Sustainable development

4 Mixtures
- Mixtures and states of matter
- Homogeneous and heterogeneous mixtures
- Magnetic separation
- Filtration
- Evaporation and distillation

5 Chemical reactions
- Characteristics of chemical reactions
- Combustion
- Oxidation
- Fermentation

6 Magnetism
- Magnets and magnetism
- Magnetic fields
- Attraction and repulsion
- The Earth's magnetic field
- Electromagnets

Projects and experiments	Documentaries
• Create a comic book about the nervous system • Investigate how the brain can affect our reflexes	• Sensing our world
• Record a podcast about advances in science • Find out how bacteria are spread	• Working together: look what your body can do
• Plan a sustainable city • Discover how plants react to different liquids	• Sustainability is the future
• Experiment with mixtures and create a poster • Investigate how chromatography works	• Messy and not so messy mixtures
• Write a report about chemical reactions and create a class magazine • Discover how important oxygen is for combustion	• Different reactions
• Design and demonstrate a magnetism experiment for a science fair • Investigate the relationship between electricity and magnetism	• It's all about the field

Extra activities  Page 90

WHO ARE THESE GREAT SCIENTISTS?

These scientists have used science to improve our lives, but science is easy for anyone to use, including you. The most important quality to have is curiosity!

Before reading the text, can you guess what each scientist did?

2 Dorothy Crowfoot Hodgkin

She used X-rays to determine what certain molecules look like, e.g. penicillin, vitamin B12 and insulin.

1 Linda B. Buck

She worked out how the receptors in our noses enable us to sense so many different smells. You should think of her the next time you smell something delicious!

3 Rosalind Franklin

She carried out the first X-rays of genetic material, which allowed other scientists to discover the structure of DNA. Now we know that DNA is arranged in a spiral!

Which scientist is being described? Listen and guess.

Did you know _____ discovered … ?

Their work was important because …

4

4 Marie Curie

She discovered and studied the radioactive elements radium and polonium. These became important in other scientific experiments and in medicine, to treat tumours.

5 Louis Pasteur

The vaccines he developed have saved many lives and protected millions of people. He found ways to make our food safer to eat.

6 Hans Christian Ørsted

He demonstrated the relationship between electricity and magnetism, using an electrical circuit to move a magnetised compass needle. This is now known as the Ørsted experiment and it's so easy you can do it at home!

You!

Starting with the fascinating topics you will learn about this year, how can you use your curiosity to contribute to science?

Can you name any other famous scientists?
What discoveries have they made?

Our senses allow us to appreciate and interact with our environment. We could not survive without them! Our nervous system enables us to interpret the information from the senses and react.

Look and discuss...

Which senses are being used? How?

1

2

We use our ... to ...

... is being used to ...

3

4
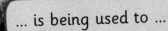

1 taste; 2 sight; 3 smell; 4 sight and hearing; 5 sight and touch; 6 hearing

S⊙ng
See, hear, touch, smell, taste

> I'm Super Sensational Girl! I'll help you learn how we interact with our environment and how our nervous system works.

Can you think of ways our senses help us escape danger?

D⊳CUMENTARY
Sensing our world

Explore

Invent a superhero and make a comic book about the nervous system. You will:
- learn how our bodies detect and respond to stimuli.
- understand the pathways of the nervous system.
- imagine life without one of your senses and develop empathy and respect for others.
- create a visual and written comic book relating to a sense and a reaction.

Interaction begins with our **sense organs**. These contain **receptors**, which are specialised cells that collect information, known as **stimuli**, from all around us. This information is then passed on to the **nervous system**.

SIGHT

Organ: eye

Receptors: in the retina

Stimulus: reflected light

Nerve: optic

eyelid

iris

retina

pupil

cornea

lens

optic nerve

Humans have five main sense organs. Each one is sensitive to a different type of **stimulus**.

How does the eye work? Find some videos! Make a labelled model and write a description.

TOUCH

Organ: skin

Receptors: in the dermis

Stimulus: pressure, texture, heat, pain

Nerve: many sensory nerves in the peripheral nervous system

hair

dermis

blood vessel

nerve receptor

HEARING

Organ: ear

Receptors: in the cochlea

Stimulus: sound waves

Nerve: auditory

Investigate how sound waves reach the nervous system through the ear.

outer ear

auditory canal

auditory nerve

cochlea

eardrum

middle ear

SMELL

Organ: nose

Receptors: cells inside nostrils

Stimulus: chemicals in the air

Nerve: olfactory

nerve receptors

olfactory nerve

nose

nasal cavity

tongue

taste buds

gustatory nerve

TASTE

Organ: tongue

Receptors: cells in taste buds

Stimulus: chemicals in food

Nerve: gustatory

Can you name the different types of taste?

A lot of what we taste comes from smelling our food. When our nose is blocked, the chemicals cannot reach the receptor cells in our nostrils which affects our sense of taste as well.

Design and carry out an experiment to test this!

Explore   STAGE 1

- Choose a stimulus for your superhero. For example, they see something dangerous or hear someone shouting from far away. This will be their *super sense*.
- Find out how humans detect this stimulus. What receptors and organs are used?
- Create the first scene for your comic book. Draw and write about the sense, receptors and organs involved.

DO PARTS OF OUR BRAIN CONTROL DIFFERENT THINGS?

Discover...

how the nervous system works.

Our nervous system is our body's control centre. It interprets all the information we receive and tells our body what to do.

Like other systems, the nervous system is made up of cells, tissues and organs. The smallest part is a nerve cell, or **neuron**.

brain

nerves

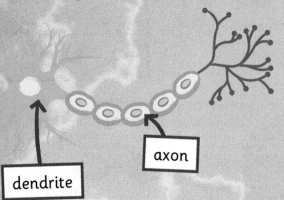

dendrite

axon

spinal cord

The **dendrites** in neurons are often the receptors from our sense organs. They transform a stimulus into an electrical signal, called an **impulse**. Once an impulse is started, it is sent along the **axons** of the neurons, through the body.

Nerve impulses can travel at speeds of 70 metres per second! Find out how and why.

There are three main types of neuron within the nervous system:

Key:
- central nervous system
- peripheral nervous system

sensory neurons: carry signals from receptors to the spinal cord and brain.

interneurons: carry signals between the different parts of the central nervous system.

motor neurons: carry signals from the central nervous system to effectors. Where in the body can you find each type of neuron?

The nervous system is divided into two parts: the **central nervous system** and the **peripheral nervous system**.

Look at the illustration. What does each part include?

The **spinal cord** is nerve tissue that runs down our spine. It connects the nerves to our brain. It also controls reflexes.

The **brain** decodes the information from nerve impulses and decides if a response is needed. It coordinates a **response** with motor neurons.

Each part of the brain controls different processes.

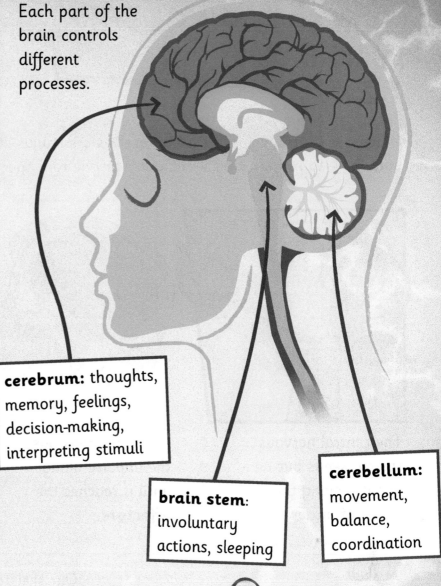

cerebrum: thoughts, memory, feelings, decision-making, interpreting stimuli

brain stem: involuntary actions, sleeping

cerebellum: movement, balance, coordination

Find out more about what the brain controls and draw a brain map.

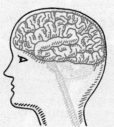

Find another brain hidden in the unit.

Explore STAGE 2

- Think about your superhero's super sense. How does it reach the central nervous system?
- Create the next scenes for your comic book and include written descriptions. Remember to use connectors.
- Show the stimulus travelling along neurons and reaching the central nervous system.

Then, …

Next, …

Afterwards, …

Finally, …

HOW DO GYMNASTS BEND BACKWARDS?

Discover...

the parts of the musculoskeletal system.

When our central nervous system receives a stimulus, it tells our body how to **respond** by sending a message to a specific part.

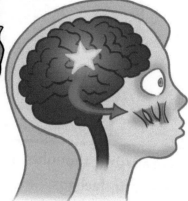

The central nervous system sends out an impulse along the axons of motor neurons.

Motor neurons pass the impulse along until it reaches the **effectors**.

Effectors include the parts of our **musculoskeletal system**. This is made up of our **skeleton** and **muscles**, which work together to allow us to move.

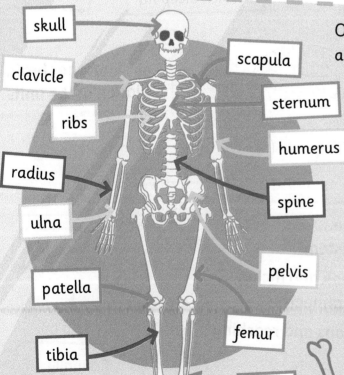

- skull
- clavicle
- ribs
- radius
- ulna
- patella
- tibia
- scapula
- sternum
- humerus
- spine
- pelvis
- femur
- fibula

Our skeleton supports our body and protects our inner organs.

What are bones made of?

Do they have another function?

A **joint** is where two bones are connected. There are three types:

Fixed, like the parts of the skull.

Semi-flexible, like in the spine.

Flexible, like in the knee.

Which joints allow a gymnast to do this?

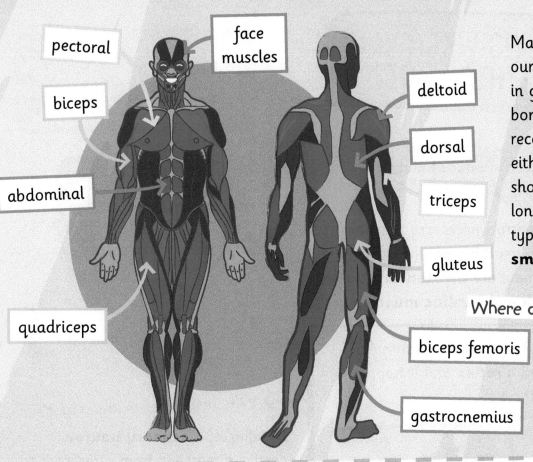

pectoral

face muscles

biceps

abdominal

quadriceps

deltoid

dorsal

triceps

gluteus

biceps femoris

gastrocnemius

Many of the muscles in our body work together in groups to move our bones. When a muscle receives a stimulus, it either **contracts** (gets shorter) or **relaxes** (gets longer). There are three types of muscle: **skeletal**, **smooth** and **cardiac**.

Where do you find each type?

Find out how our skeletal muscles attach to our bones.

Some muscles work in pairs, like the biceps and triceps muscles. When one muscle contracts, the opposite muscle relaxes.

Try it yourself! Describe the changes happening.

What is the fastest muscle in your body? If you blink, you might miss it.

biceps

triceps

lower arm

Explore — STAGE 3

- Find out which muscles and bones are involved in the response related to your superhero's initial stimulus.
- Discuss with a partner and compare the pathways of your super senses!
- Create some scenes to show the pathway and the response. Include pictures and written descriptions.

My pathway includes the ...

It travels along the motor neurons in the ... to the ...

WHAT HAPPENS WHEN YOU TOUCH SOMETHING HOT?

Discover...

how reflexes work and keep us safe.

Most of the actions involving our **skeletal muscles** are **voluntary**.

Our nervous system controls necessary functions that keep us alive, like breathing and heart rate, without us thinking. These are **involuntary** actions carried out by **smooth** and **cardiac muscles**.

Sometimes a very quick response to a stimulus is needed. This is called a **reflex** and it happens without us having to think.

OUCH!

→ Why are reflexes important?

In reflexes, a **sensory neuron** carries a message from a receptor to the **spinal cord**. A **motor neuron** carries the response message back to an effector. The brain is not involved. This is called a **reflex arc**.

Find out about other reflexes!

Explore — STAGE 3

- Imagine you no longer have one of your senses. What would your life be like?
- Find out about people who live without your superhero's sense. Discuss with a partner.
- To add drama to your comic, your superhero could lose their super sense. What happens? Include scenes to show this and add a paragraph to explain.

Look back...

Is it quicker for an impulse to reach the brain or the spinal cord? Why is this important for reflexes?

People who cannot ... are ....

They manage without ... by ...

WHY DOES A TENNIS PLAYER MOVE WHILE WAITING FOR A SERVE?

Discover...

how reflexes can be affected.

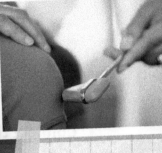
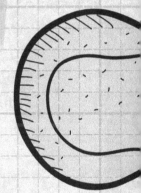

Background: When the knee is tapped, the patellar reflex makes the lower leg move. But sometimes the brain can get in the way of a reflex, changing the reaction.

Hypothesis: When your brain is activated, will your response to the stimulus be more, less, or the same?

Materials: table or desk, your hand

Step 1: Ask your partner to sit so their legs hang freely. Find the soft indent below the patella on one of your partner's knees. With your palm facing up, gently tap them in this spot with the side of your hand.

Step 2: In the same position, have your partner lock their fingers together and ask them to try to pull their hands apart. Gently tap their knee again.

Reflect 1

What is the response? Which muscles are responsible? Draw a picture.

Reflect 2

What is the response now? How does it compare to the response in Step 1?

Conclusion: How can you explain the difference in the response?

How could this knowledge be useful to athletes?

When our brain is activated, our reflexes are ...

Athletes should ... to react ... to a stimulus.

Language Review

1 In your notebook, match the adjectives with a preposition to complete the sentences.

> attached bad good keen sensitive   for on to

a Muscles are ..... bones by tendons.
b I'm not very ..... working out to build my muscles.
c Reading in poor light is ..... your eyes because it tires your irises.
d Our nostrils have receptors that are ..... chemicals in the air.
e Doing exercise is ..... your health.

2 Connect the sentences using *so* or *nor*. Use the example to help you.

a The brain receives stimuli from receptors in the sense organs. The spinal cord receives stimuli from receptors in the sense organs.
   The brain receives stimuli from receptors in the sense organs and so does the spinal cord.
b Blind people cannot experience one of their senses. Deaf people cannot experience one of their senses.
c Muscles are effectors. Bones are also effectors.
d Jill has a great sense of smell. I have a great sense of smell, too.
e Ben does not like the taste of sweet and sour meatballs. We do not love the taste of sweet and sour meatballs either.

3 🎧 You will hear a woman telling a group of people about someone who is lacking a sense. Write the correct answer in your notebook for each gap.

> ### Colour blindness
>
> It is difficult for colour-blind people to tell the difference between green and (a) ..... or yellow and (b) ..... .
>
> Mike, who is colour blind, cannot distinguish between (c) ..... and ripe tomatoes.
>
> (d) ..... percent of boys have colour vision problems, which is more than girls.
>
> Colour vision problems occur when receptors in the retina do not respond to the colour variations in (e) ..... .
>
> To test for colour blindness, people are asked to identify the (f) ..... they see inside a circle.

1 Take turns answering the questions with a partner. The person with the most points wins.

Partner A:

a What are the five main senses?

b Name three parts of the eye.

c What is a joint?

d What is the central nervous system?

e Name at least five muscles.

Partner B:

a What are the names of the five sense organs?

b Name three parts of the ear.

c What is a reflex arc?

d What is the peripheral nervous system?

e Name at least five bones.

2 What is happening in the photos? Write a description.

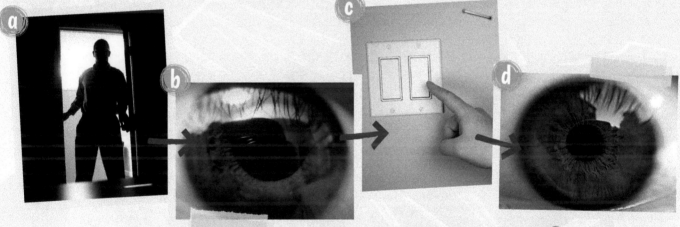

Assessment link

For more Unit 1 activities go to page 78.

 **FINALE**

- Create the final scene to complete your comic. Include a drawing and write a paragraph.

- Make a title page for your comic and think of a catchy title!

- Present your comic to your classmates in small groups.

Meet my superhero: ... !

Prepare for an adventure with ... !

2 NUTRITION

All living things need nutrients to live and grow. Our systems must work together to process these nutrients and to expel waste and harmful substances. This is called nutrition. It is a continuous process!

Look and discuss...

Which systems are involved in nutrition? What does each system do?

When we ..., we use our ... system.

1

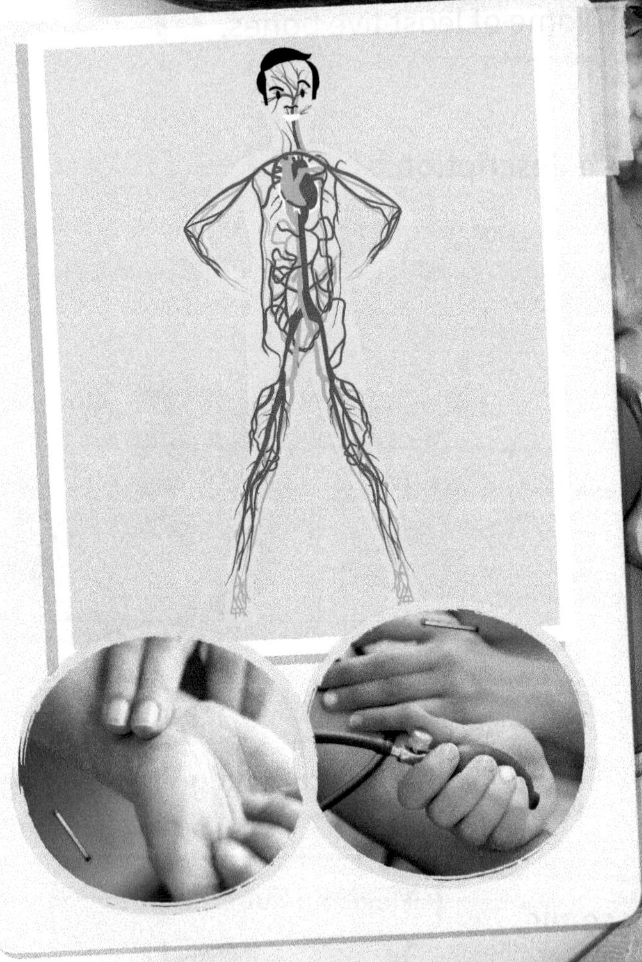

2

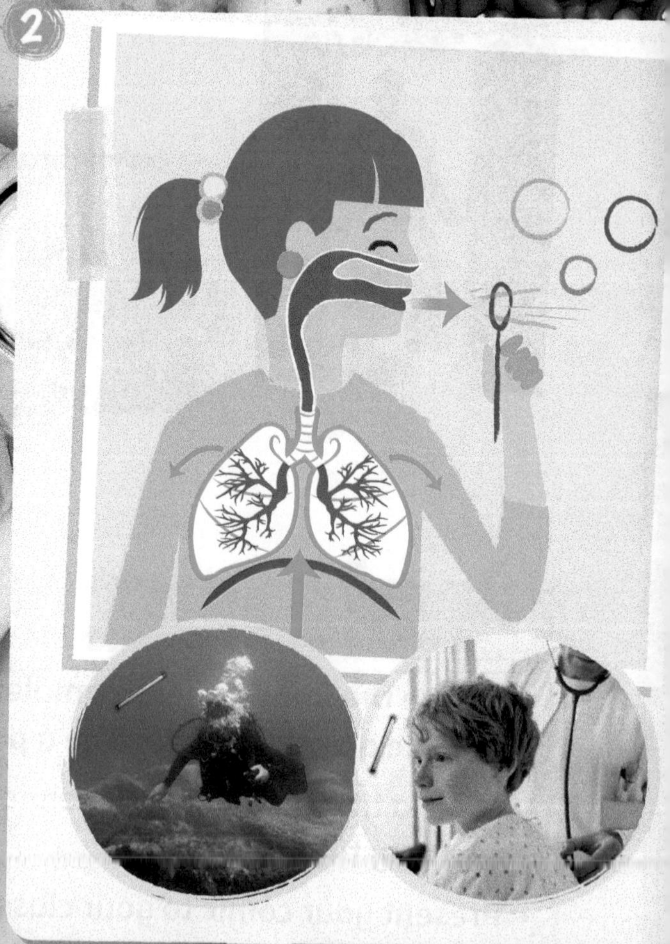

1 circulatory system: delivers nutrients and oxygen; 2 respiratory system: brings in oxygen, expels carbon dioxide; 3 digestive system: takes in and processes food; 4 excretory system: removes waste

Our ... system enables us to ...

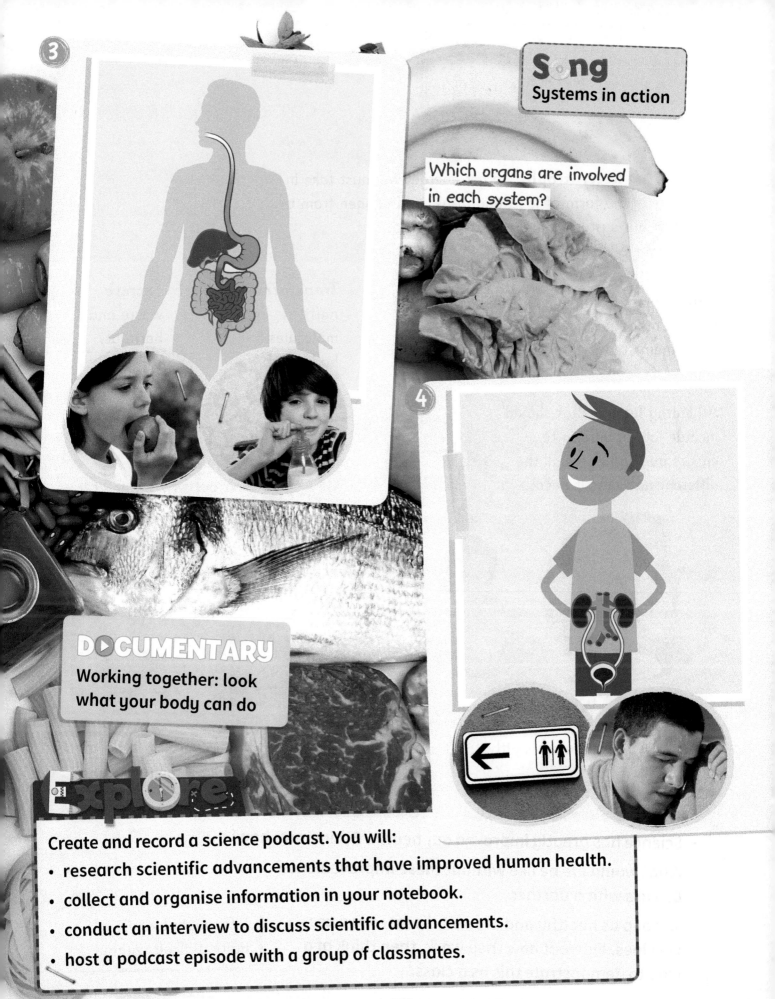

③

Which organs are involved in each system?

④

D▶CUMENTARY
Working together: look what your body can do

Explore

Create and record a science podcast. You will:

- research scientific advancements that have improved human health.
- collect and organise information in your notebook.
- conduct an interview to discuss scientific advancements.
- host a podcast episode with a group of classmates.

WHY SHOULD WE EAT HEALTHY FOOD?

Discover...

the principle stages of human nutrition.

Humans are **heterotrophs**. To get energy, we must take in nutrients in the form of food and drink, and oxygen from the air. Then our systems do all of the hard work!

Nutrition is a simple process made up of three main steps:

1 Take in nutrients, like food, vitamins and oxygen.

2 Transform nutrients into molecules our bodies can use.

3 Excrete waste and harmful substances.

A healthy human **diet** should include lots of variety to ensure our body gets all the different nutrients it needs.

Breathing in **oxygen** is another vital part of our nutrition.

Find out why we need it and the role it plays in nutrition.

Who is eating healthy food?

What do you do to keep healthy? Tell a partner.

Why is breathing in polluted air not good for us?

Explore STAGE 1

- Science has greatly improved our health. Brainstorm how!
- What would life be like without these improvements? Discuss with a partner.
- To keep us healthy and prevent diseases, we use vaccines. Find out how they work, then think of a way to demonstrate this as a class.

Life would be easier / more difficult without ...

ARE CARROTS GOOD FOR OUR EYES?

Our bodies are machines that are constantly working to keep us **healthy**. Like any machine, we must take care of it! To function properly, the body needs to take in certain substances and get rid of waste.

Carbohydrates, like starch, sugar and fibre, give us energy.

Fats give us energy and provide protection.

Take in:

- food
  - carbohydrates
  - proteins
  - fats
  - vitamins and minerals
- water
- oxygen

Remove:

- solid waste
- carbon dioxide
- urea
- toxins

How do our bodies get rid of these substances?

Like building blocks, **proteins** make up our tissues and organs.

Proteins keep you strong!

Vitamins and **minerals** are vital for many small, but important jobs. They help our immune system, help us grow and help our cells work properly.

You need lots of vitamins to see, so carrots are very good for you!

8   15.999
O
Oxygen

Our bodies use **water** in many different ways.

Find out more!

All our cells need **oxygen** to transform carbohydrates into energy.

HOW DOES FOOD MOVE THROUGH OUR BODY?

Discover...

the organs involved in the digestive system.

The **digestive system** breaks down the food we take in and works with other systems to extract the nutrients and expel undigested waste. **Digestion** begins in our mouth as soon as we start eating.

Follow the digestion pathway with your finger. Can you describe what each part does?

1
- **Saliva** production begins when we smell food.
- **Teeth** crush food as we chew.
- Food is shaped into a ball by the **tongue**.

Why is saliva necessary?

2
- Food is passed into the **oesophagus** when we swallow.
- The **epiglottis** stops food going down the windpipe.
- Muscles contract to send the food down to the stomach.

Find out about the role bacteria play in human digestion.

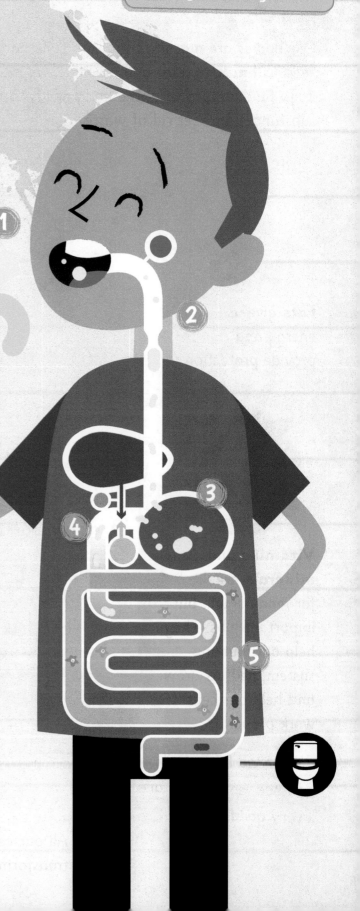

3

- The **stomach** is made of strong muscles.
- Food is broken down into small pieces here.
- **Gastric juices** mix with the food.

Many animals have weird digestive systems. Find out about a lobster's teeth or a giraffe's stomach.

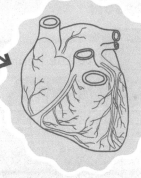

What do gastric juices do?

4

- When it is liquid, food is passed into the **small intestine**.
- It is mixed with **bile** from the **liver** and **pancreatic fluid** from the **pancreas**.
- This breaks the mixture down into different types of nutrients.
- Afterwards, **absorption** occurs, and nutrients are passed into the blood.

Can you name the organ that stores the bile?

Can you name the different types of nutrients?

5

- Undigested waste continues through the **large intestine**.
- Water **reabsorption** into the blood occurs.
- Solid waste passes through the **rectum** and leaves our body through the **anus**.

Why is the heart important here?

Look back

What types of muscle are in the digestive system?

 Explore — STAGE 2

- Food allergies are very serious, but EpiPens can save lives. How?
- Laparoscopy is a cool, new technology. Learn more about it.
- Type 1 diabetes is a disease that affects the pancreas. Research the discovery of insulin and its importance.
- Decide how to organise this information in your notebook. Include photos or drawings.

WHAT IS BLOOD MADE OF?

Discover...

how the circulatory system works.

The **circulatory system** delivers nutrients and oxygen to all the cells and tissues in the body. It has three main parts: the blood, the blood vessels and the heart.

Blood

- Red liquid.
- Transports oxygen, carbon dioxide and nutrients around the body.
- Made up of cells with different functions.

    Find out more about what each type of cell does.

red blood cell

white blood cell

platelet

plasma

Blood vessels

Arteries carry blood with oxygen away from the heart and around the body.

Capillaries connect the arteries and veins together and allow for gas exchange.

Veins carry blood with carbon dioxide back to the heart.

Are all blood vessels the same size? Give examples.

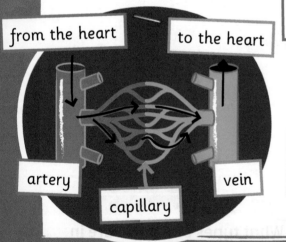

from the heart

to the heart

artery

vein

capillary

Heart

- A muscular organ with four chambers.
- Pumps blood around the body.

    Why do you hear two sounds when you listen to your heart?

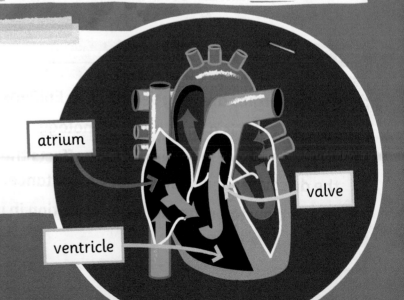

atrium

valve

ventricle

Blood flows around the body in two loops. This is called **circulation**.

- **Pulmonary loop:**
  Blood flows from the heart to the lungs and then back to the heart. It expels carbon dioxide and picks up oxygen.

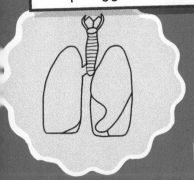

heart

veins

capillaries

deoxygenated blood

 arteries

lungs

- **Systemic loop:**
  Blood flows from the heart to the rest of the body. It delivers oxygen to all the cells and tissues and picks up carbon dioxide and waste.

oxygenated blood

Oxygenated blood flows past the small intestine to pick up nutrients and delivers them to the rest of the body.

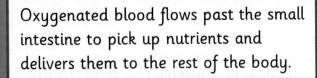 STAGE 3

- Do some research about transplants and electrocardiography (ECG).
- Why are these important for the circulatory system?
- Nowadays, smartwatches use ECG technology. Draw an example of an ECG in your notebook. Tell a partner what the peaks mean.

WHAT ARE ALVEOLI?

Discover...

what the respiratory and excretory systems do.

The **respiratory system** is the body's gas exchange centre. It brings oxygen into the body and lets carbon dioxide out. The respiratory system is closely connected to the **excretory system**, which eliminates waste and keeps us cool.

Inhalation

Exhalation

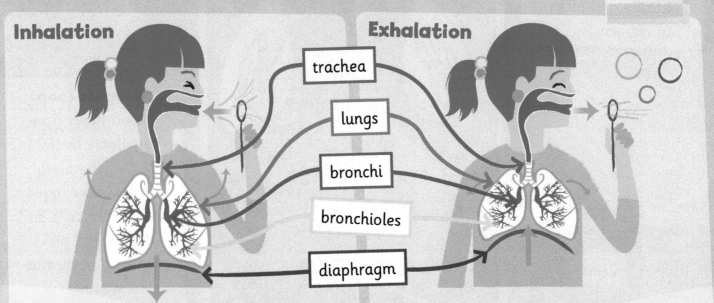

trachea

lungs

bronchi

bronchioles

diaphragm

- The diaphragm (the large muscle under your lungs) **contracts** and lowers.
- The lungs **inflate**.
- Oxygen flows from nose and mouth
  - trachea ➡ bronchi ➡ bronchioles
  - alveoli ➡ blood vessels.

- The diaphragm **relaxes** and rises.
- The lungs **deflate**.
- Carbon dioxide flows from blood vessels
  - alveoli ➡ bronchioles ➡ bronchi
  - trachea ➡ nose and mouth.

The **lungs** are shaped like upside down trees, with the **airways** becoming smaller and smaller until they reach tiny 'balloons' called **alveoli**. Alveoli are surrounded by capillaries.

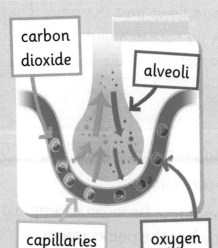

carbon dioxide

alveoli

capillaries

oxygen

Once oxygen is in the blood, the circulatory system carries it to the rest of the body, including the brain.

You have more than 300 million alveoli in each lung. Why do you need so many?

What are hiccups? Find out!

Which part of the nervous system controls breathing?

As our body uses energy, it produces toxins that need to be removed.

All blood passes through the **renal arteries** in our **kidneys** where the blood is filtered. This produces **urine**, which is waste mixed with water.

Where does urine travel next? Where is it stored?

Why is it important to drink lots of water each day? Find out about kidney stones.

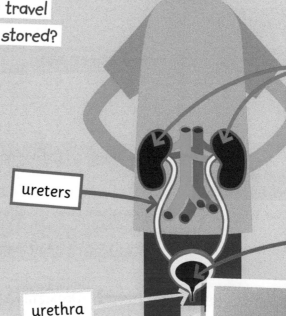

kidneys

ureters

bladder

urethra

sweat gland

Our **skin** is also part of the excretory system. **Sweat glands** in the skin excrete **sweat**, a mixture of water and salts, through **pores**. When sweat evaporates from the skin, it cools us down.

Explore   STAGE 4

- **Do you know anyone with asthma? Do they use an inhaler? Find out more.**
- **When a kidney stops functioning, dialysis can save someone's life. Learn more about it.**
- **Add the information to your notebook.**

WHAT SHOULD YOU DO IN AN EMERGENCY?

Discover...

basic first-aid techniques.

An emergency can be frightening, but you must try to **stay calm**.

Remember:
- ✓ Stay calm.
- ✓ Stay safe.
- ✓ Get help.
- ✗ Do not do anything dangerous.

If someone is hurt, first aid could help.

What should you do if ...

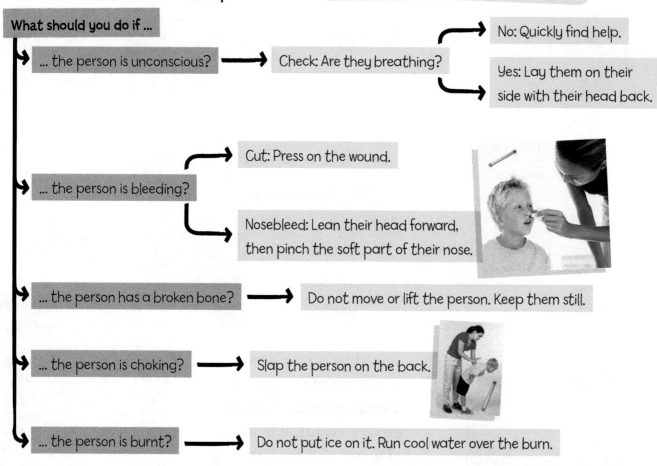

... the person is unconscious? → Check: Are they breathing?

No: Quickly find help.

Yes: Lay them on their side with their head back.

... the person is bleeding?

Cut: Press on the wound.

Nosebleed: Lean their head forward, then pinch the soft part of their nose.

... the person has a broken bone? → Do not move or lift the person. Keep them still.

... the person is choking? → Slap the person on the back.

... the person is burnt? → Do not put ice on it. Run cool water over the burn.

As soon as you can, find an adult to help you.

What would you include in a first-aid kit? Discuss with a partner.

STAGE 5

- Medical advancements in science have improved everyone's lives. In pairs, prepare an interview and discuss one of the advancements you have researched during the unit.

- Write down questions and possible responses to create a script for a podcast.

In what ways has science helped you?

Science has changed my life because ...

HOW IMPORTANT IS IT TO WASH YOUR HANDS?

Find Out more...

Discover...

how bacteria can affect our health.

Background: For centuries people did not know that microorganisms caused diseases because they were so small. Scientists now understand how the spread of germs is linked to cleanliness. This discovery is known as the **germ theory**.

Hypothesis: Do clean hands have more or less bacteria? Why?

Materials: 250ml boiling water, two packets of gelatine, beef stock cube, two teaspoons of sugar, measuring jug, spoon, two shallow dishes, plastic wrap, two cotton swabs

Step 1: Make agar by mixing the water, gelatine, stock cube and sugar in a bowl. Pour half into each shallow dish. Cover with plastic wrap and place in the fridge overnight.

Step 2: Remove the plastic wrap from one of the dishes. Scrape a cotton swab on your left hand and then run it gently along the top of the agar. Replace the plastic wrap. Mark this dish as the control.

Step 3: Wash your hands with soap and water for 20 seconds. Use a different cotton swab and repeat Step 2 with the other dish.

Step 4: Observe the dishes over the next few days and record the results.

Reflect 1

What are the gelatine, stock cube and sugar for?

Reflect 2

Which dish has more bacteria growth? Is it the same colour?

Washing our hands can ...

We can prevent disease by ...

Conclusion: How important is it to wash our hands? Why?

Find something we use to wash our hands hidden in the unit.

Who would benefit from this information?

1 Complete the sentences in your notebook.

a You should always check the breathing of someone ..... is unconscious.

b The stomach, ... main job is to break down food, is connected to the oesophagus and the small intestine.

c The lungs are different sizes: the lung ..... is smaller is on the left.

d Sweat glands in the skin excrete sweat, ... is a mixture of water and salts.

e My grandma, ... is 97 years old, never eats fast food.

2 Use comparatives and superlatives to complete the sentences.

a We absorb ..... nutrients in our small intestine.

b We need ..... fat ..... protein for a healthy diet.

c With antibiotics, diseases are ..... harmful ... they used to be.

d We need ..... carbohydrates ..... vitamins for a healthy diet.

e Our washed hands have ..... bacteria.

3 🎧 Listen to a radio programme about penicillin. For each question, choose the correct answer.

1 Penicillin is used to kill:

  a viruses.

  b bacteria.

  c fungi.

2 Who discovered penicillin?

  a The ancient Egyptians.

  b Alexander Fleming.

  c Howard Florey.

3 How was penicillin discovered?

  a A baker was trying a new recipe.

  b A scientist found mould on a dish.

  c A dishwasher found mould on a plate.

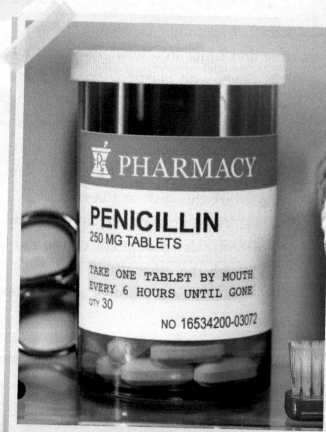

1 Write the names of the organs and the system they belong to. What is the role of each organ in nutrition?

2 Order the sentences.

a The circulatory system carries nutrients around the body to different tissues and picks up waste.

b The excretory system filters the blood and removes the waste from the body.

c In the small intestine, nutrients are absorbed into the blood.

d Nutrients from food are taken in and digested by the digestive system.

Assessment link

For more Unit 2 activities go to page 80.

FINALE

- In groups, record a podcast where you discuss the scientific advancements you have researched. Be sure to reflect on what life was like before they were discovered.

- Decide who will be the host, who will be on the panel of experts and who will participate in an interview. Think about what each person could talk about and in what order.

- Be creative and fun. Your listeners should be entertained!

There didn't use to be …

Nowadays, science allows us to …

3

WE ARE NATURE

Look and discuss...

What natural resources are being used and how?

We often forget it, but humans are part of the natural environment. Just like other living things, we must interact with our surroundings to survive. However, unlike most living things, humans have managed to completely change the natural environment to meet their needs. How might this affect other living things?

Which kingdoms can you identify in these photos?

Other living things for food (1, 7, 8, 9) or entertainment (5, 8); water for entertainment (2, 8); water for growing plants (3, 7); water for drinking and electricity (6); plants for materials (4)

5

6

What non-living things do humans use from nature?

7

8

9

We use ... for ...

... allows us to ...

Are all these places natural?

Explore

Plan a sustainable city. You will:

- Find out about the organisms that live in your local area and how they use water.
- Discover where your drinking water comes from.
- Learn about sustainable development and how it can be applied to your local area.
- Persuade your classmates to be more sustainable.

TO WHICH KINGDOM DO HUMANS BELONG?

All living things are classified into five **kingdoms** that share certain characteristics, like nutrition and reproduction. Organisms from different kingdoms also interact with each another.

Discover...

the main characteristics of the five kingdoms.

Organisms that get nutrients by consuming other organisms.

One individual reproduces by copying its genetic material.

1 Monera kingdom

Nutrition: **heterotrophs**

Reproduction: **asexual**

Also known as bacteria, these are simple, unicellular organisms. Bacteria can live on any surface on Earth where there is liquid. Although we often think of them as dangerous, they're really important and can even be helpful!

What role do bacteria and fungi play in every ecosystem?

Genetic material from two organisms combines to produce a new living organism.

2 Fungi kingdom

Nutrition: heterotrophs

Reproduction: asexual and **sexual**

This kingdom includes **unicellular** yeasts and **multicellular** mushrooms, but the main thing fungi have in common is their ability to break down other organisms.

What does marine coral have in common with a bird?

Some animals are herbivores, some carnivores, and others omnivores. Give an example of each.

3 Animal kingdom

Nutrition: heterotrophs

Reproduction: mostly sexual; a few asexual

Ranging from simple to complex, all animals are multicellular. They consume other living things to survive. This kingdom is divided into two groups, **vertebrates** and **invertebrates**, both of which are divided into subgroups with similar traits.

What do these three kingdoms have in common?

Can you make a list of these with a partner?

What protists can you find at the beach?

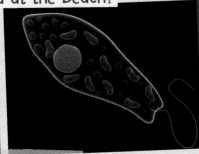

4 Protist kingdom

Nutrition: **autotrophs** and heterotrophs

Reproduction: asexual and sexual

The organisms in this kingdom, which include **algae** and **protozoans**, don't have any unifying traits! Some are unicellular and make their own food, others are multicellular hunters. Most move using flagella or by amoeboid movement, but some are nonmotile.

What process do plants use to make their own food?

These are divided into flowering and non-flowering plants.

5 Plant kingdom

Nutrition: autotrophs

Reproduction: mainly sexual

Without this kingdom, most life on Earth couldn't survive. In any ecosystem, plants are the main **producers** because they make their own food. Plants are multicellular and have **cell walls** and vacuoles.

The kingdom is divided into two types: **non-vasuclar**, plants without xylem; and **vascular**, plants with xylem. Can you name an example of each?

Which of these **instruments** can you use to observe organisms from different kingdoms? Experiment with a partner!

It's fun to observe living things, but we should respect and care for them and their habitats. How can you do this?

Explore   STAGE 1

- **Draw a map of your town or city, including the surroundings and waterways. Label the natural, industrial, agricultural and urban areas.**

- **What other organisms live in your area? Use the internet to make a list.**

- **How many of these organisms have you seen? Go on a walking tour and tick the organisms you see.**

- **Where did you see the most organisms?**

Like me, ... live in an urban/rural ecosystem.

Most organisms in a city live near ...

35

DO PLANTS DRINK WATER?

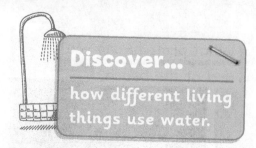
Life on Earth depends on a vital substance: **water**. Without it, living things could not survive. Wherever you find water on Earth, from the deepest ocean to the top of the tallest mountain, you will find living things.

Different organisms use **water** in different ways:

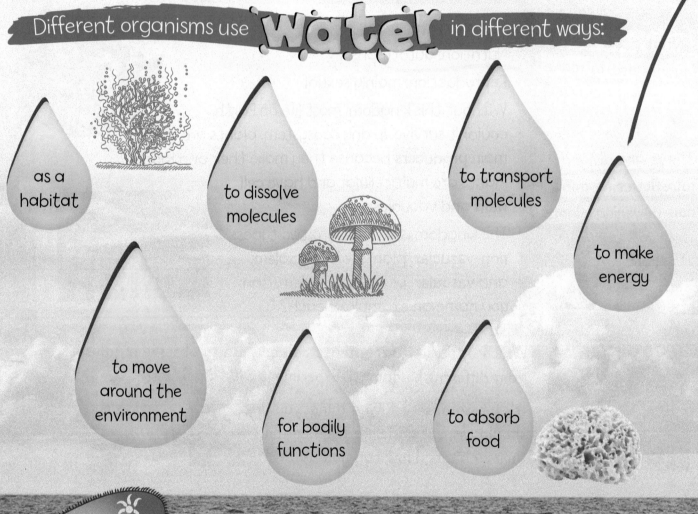

as a habitat

to dissolve molecules

to transport molecules

to make energy

to move around the environment

for bodily functions

to absorb food

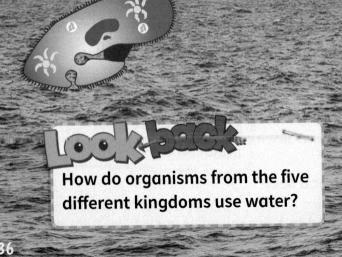

Look back

How do organisms from the five different kingdoms use water?

Try this ...

Collect a sample of water from a nearby pond, stream or puddle. Observe it under a **microscope** and draw the organisms you see. Which kingdoms do they belong to? Use the internet to help you.

Water is so important for life because it allows organisms to create the **energy** they need to carry out vital body functions.

Why does NASA say 'follow the water' in the search for extra-terrestrial life?

In each of their cells, heterotrophs use water to break down sugar and release energy.

Plants, and other autotrophs, use water for **photosynthesis**.

1 Water and minerals are taken up by the **roots** of plants from the soil.

2 They move up the stem through the **xylem**, which act as the plant's veins.

3 The water and minerals reach the plant's **leaves**. This is where photosynthesis occurs. Carbon dioxide enters through the tiny **stomata**, while light energy is absorbed by **chlorophyll**, a green pigment.

4 Light energy is used to combine the carbon dioxide with the water and minerals, which produces **glucose**. Oxygen is also produced and released into the air.

5 **Phloem** transports the glucose to other parts of the plant where it can be used to grow.

Oxygen

Carbon dioxide

Glucose (sugar)

Water and minerals

Water enters leaf

Light energy

Carbon dioxide enters leaf through stomata

Sugar leaves leaf

How does dirty or polluted water affect plants?

Explore STAGE 2

- Look at your list of local organisms and mark them on your map. How does each one use water?

- How do you use water? Make a water journal and record all the ways you use water in a day.

- Compare your list with a partner. Are they similar?

... use water to ...

I couldn't ... without water.

CAN PLANTS GROW IN JUICE?

Discover...
how plants react to different amounts of water.

Background: To carry out photosynthesis, plants need water. However, they are very **adaptable**. They can sometimes obtain water from other liquids that contain water.

Hypothesis: Can a plant still grow in liquids that are not water? Why? / Why not?

Materials: five carrots, five plates, water, milk, juice, sports drink, measuring cup, ruler

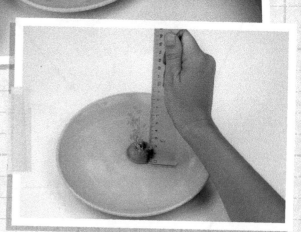

Step 1: Label each plate with numbers 1–5. Cut the top off each carrot and place on separate plates.

Step 2: Do not pour any liquid on plate 1. On each of the other plates, pour 150ml of either water, milk, juice and sports drink. You will need to repeat this step after a few days so that they don't dry out.

Step 3: Wait seven days. Does a new stem grow from each carrot? If so, measure it.

Step 4: Keep measuring every day for one more week.

Reflect 1
Which carrot is the control? Why?

Reflect 2
Which plant grows better?

Conclusion: How did each plant react to the different liquids?

How do plants survive in places with little water?

This plant ... whereas this plant ...

I can conclude...

WHERE DOES THE WATER IN A SWIMMING POOL COME FROM?

On a hot day, have you ever wondered where all the cool water in a swimming pool comes from? Even though humans are part of the **natural environment**, we've become good at **transforming** it so that we can easily obtain water, food and protection. We even alter the environment for our entertainment!

Water is a limited **resource** because humans, like plants, need clean **freshwater** to survive. Once water is used up, we cannot produce more. It is also very difficult to clean polluted water. Therefore, we should prevent **water pollution** and never **waste** it.

Discover...

how humans adapt the environment to fill their needs ... and wants!

Where does our drinking water come from?

Although some of the water we drink is pumped up from **groundwater**, most comes from lakes and rivers. We build dams in rivers to create **reservoirs**. These are large sources of freshwater and electricity, but how do they affect local organisms?

Talk with a partner. How do these affect our drinking water, as well as the habitats of other living things?

What does the word runoff mean?

Despite only drinking freshwater, humans use salt water in many ways. How might this affect salt water habitats?

Explore   STAGE 3

- **Where does the water you use every day come from? Where does it go, as waste water, after it has been used? Use the internet or find out by contacting your local council.**

- **Record this information on your map by adding more drawings.**

Water from the tap comes from ...

After it is used, the waste water goes ...

39

IS IT TOO LATE TO SAVE THE ENVIRONMENT?

Discover...

how to care for other living things.

Although human beings can have a negative impact on the environment, it is important to remember that there are many things we can do to protect it.

1 Find and count the natural landscapes in each picture. Which has more?
2 List the ways humans have transformed the natural environment.
3 Why have humans made each of these transformations?
4 How are organisms from the five kingdoms affected in each picture?
5 List the ways that the environment is protected in picture 2.

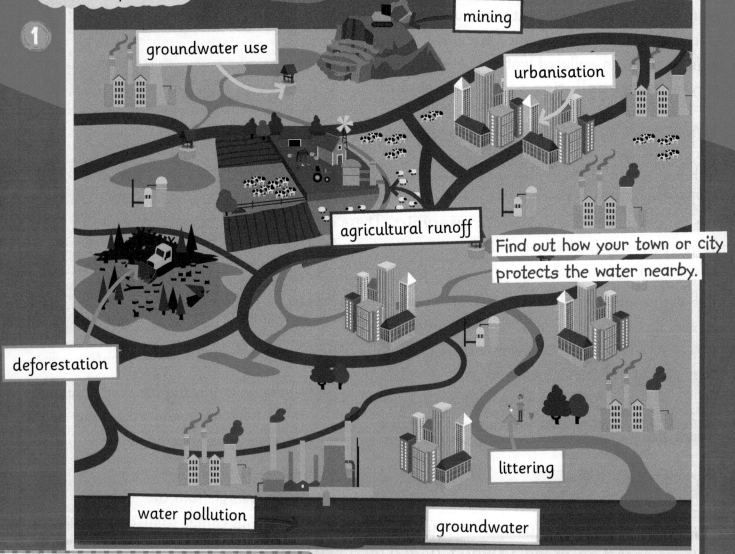

1

- mining
- groundwater use
- urbanisation
- agricultural runoff
- deforestation
- water pollution
- littering
- groundwater

Find out how your town or city protects the water nearby.

Can we clean water once it's been polluted? Listen and list the steps.

Cities produce a lot of **waste water**. If a city is near a river, all the waste will run into it unless the waste first passes through a **sewage treatment plant**.

By making a few changes, we can restore **ecological equilibrium**.

Forests and mountains give us **raw materials**. Like water, these resources must be used **sustainably** to protect them for future generations.

Find a way to save water hidden in the unit.

2 How can we prevent their depletion?

Did you know there are organisms that show us when an ecosystem is unbalanced? Find out about **bioindicators** in your local ecosystem.

Nature is good at balancing itself. However, humans can upset that **balance**.

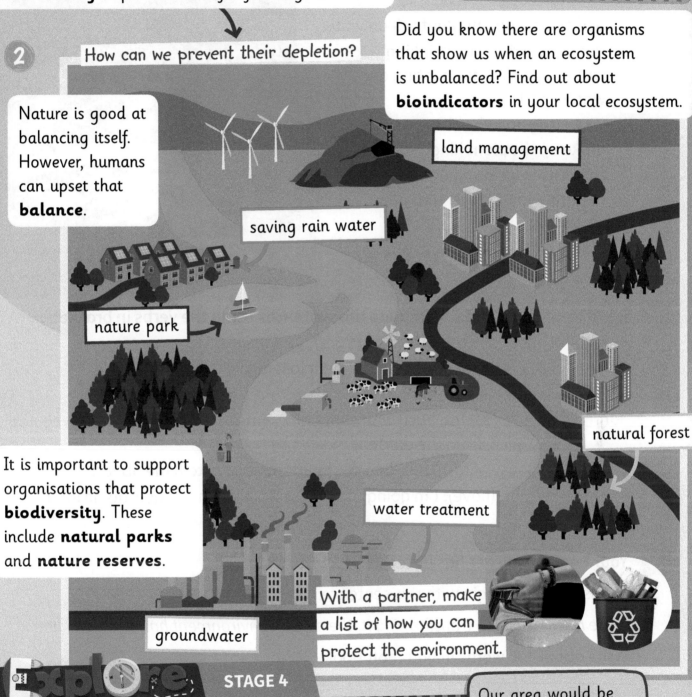

land management

saving rain water

nature park

natural forest

It is important to support organisations that protect **biodiversity**. These include **natural parks** and **nature reserves**.

water treatment

With a partner, make a list of how you can protect the environment.

groundwater

Explore   STAGE 4

Our area would be more sustainable if ...

- What is **sustainable development**? Write a definition.
- Look at the information you've gathered. How could you improve your area so it is more sustainable?
- Re-design your local area so that it is more sustainable.

If ... , then living things in our area would ...

1 **In your notebook, rewrite the sentences in passive form.**

   a Roots take up water from the soil.
     Water is taken up from the soil through roots.

   b Sewage treatment plants clean water.

   c People use rivers for drinking water, as well as for boating and water sports.

   d Flowering and non-flowering plants make up the plant kingdom.

   e Humans transform natural areas to obtain food, water and other resources.

   f Chlorophyll absorbs light energy.

2 **Read the conversation. Complete the sentences using the verbs in brackets.**

Jenny: … you … (water) the plants yet?

John: No, I … (have), but Sam … (do) it last night.

Jenny: … you … (help) her?

John: No, I … (be) too busy with supper. I … (make) a salad with fresh vegetables I … (pick) from the garden.

Jenny: … you … (finish) building the fountain you … (tell) me about?

John: Yes, I … (have). I'm going to surprise Sam when she gets home later.

3 **Your English teacher has asked you to write a story.**

Your story must begin with this sentence:

Since humans began transforming it, the natural environment has changed a lot.

Write about 100 words in your notebook.

Content Review

1 Look at the photos. Write 2–3 sentences about each kingdom using the words from the box.

asexual   sexual   autotroph   heterotroph   multicellular   unicellular

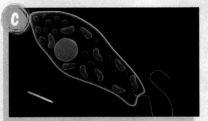

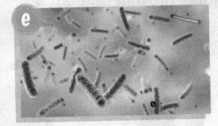

2 These photos show people in nature. Take turns to describe each one with a partner.

FINALE

- Compare your old map and your new map with a partner. Write sentences.

- Your local council (your class) is asking for applications on how to make your area more sustainable. Prepare to present your map with your sustainable development ideas.

- Convince the class to vote for your map. Use persuasive language.

- Vote on the most sustainable idea!

> As you can see, my map shows ... , which is more sustainable because ...

> This is the most sustainable way because ...

4 MIXTURES

L👓k and discuss...

**What do all these photos have in common?
Can you name the different parts?**

A mixture is a combination of two or more things that can be separated without a chemical reaction. Restaurants are not the only places where we can find mixtures.

These photos show ...

Mixtures: 1 coffee and water; 2 different fruits; 3 lettuce and tomatoes; 4 copper and nickel; 5 nuts and dried fruit; 6 oil and vinegar; 7 chocolate powder and milk; 8 bread, tomato sauce and cheese

This is made up of ...

44

5

6

7

8

Song
Mix it up!

What mixtures can you find in your classroom?

D▶CUMENTARY
Messy and not so messy mixtures

Explore

Experiment with mixtures. You will:

- understand how mixtures and their components can have different properties.
- use and evaluate different separation techniques.
- present your findings as a poster.

CAN A SOLID TRANSFORM DIRECTLY INTO A GAS?

Matter is everywhere. It is anything that takes up space and has a mass. It makes up everything around us!

Can matter be created or destroyed?
Explain your answer.

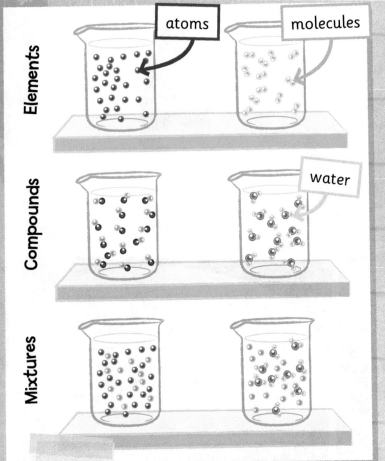

Elements — atoms — molecules

Compounds — water

Mixtures

All matter is made up of **atoms**. Atoms can join together to form **molecules**. An **element** is made up of only one type of atom.

A **pure substance** consists of all the same element or compound.

One example is water. Can you name more?

Matter can exist on its own or in a mixture. Each substance in a mixture is called a **component**. Mixtures can be made up of a few or many components, but none of the components are physically joined together.

How are compounds different from mixtures?

Find a pure substance hidden in the unit.

The **state of matter** refers to whether something is a **solid**, **liquid** or **gas** and this depends on how much energy it has.

What substance, used for special effects, changes directly from solid to gas?

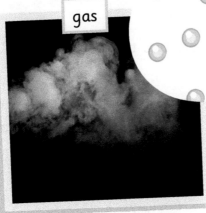

gas

What examples of changes of state can we see in the weather?

condensation

evaporation

sublimation

When matter is in a **gaseous** state, it has a lot of energy to move around. It can completely fill a container.

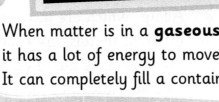

liquid

solid

solidification

melting

In a **solid** state, matter has very little energy. The molecules tend to stay in the same place and are close together.

A substance in a **liquid** state has less energy, but the molecules still move around. Liquids take the shape of their container.

Explore   STAGE 1

- Choose a mixture. Is it solid, liquid or gas? List its other properties.
- What is it composed of? Do the component properties differ from those of the mixture?
- Record the information in your notebook.

My mixture is composed of …

Some of the component properties are different / similar to …

ARE THERE NATURALLY OCCURRING MIXTURES?

Discover...

the difference between homogeneous and heterogeneous mixtures.

Based on their appearance, there are two types of mixtures.

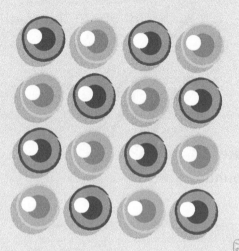

A **homogeneous** mixture has a uniform appearance. Its components are arranged in a similar way throughout. They are often made up of the same type of molecules or compounds.

Alloys, which are mixtures of different metals, are examples of homogeneous mixtures. Blood plasma, rain water and perfume are also examples.

Can you think of any others?

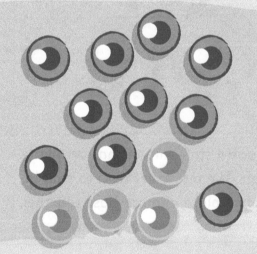

A **heterogeneous** mixture has visibly different components or states.

An example of a heterogeneous mixture is oil and vinegar.

Discuss other examples with a partner.

Look back...

Is a pure substance homogeneous or heterogeneous?

Although we can make mixtures in the kitchen or laboratory, the Earth also provides examples of mixtures.

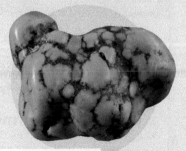

Find out about the mixtures that make up stones and gems.

CAN YOU FIND BURIED TREASURE AT THE BEACH?

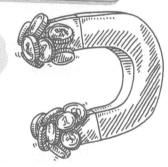

When components in a mixture are combined without a chemical reaction, they keep their own **properties**. This means they can be separated easily.

We can use **magnetism** to separate components in a mixture that display **magnetic** and **non-magnetic** properties.

Some metals, like iron and nickel, have magnetic properties. Other metals, such as gold, silver and aluminium, do not.

We can use the **attraction force** of a magnet to separate the magnetic components from the non-magnetic ones.

magnet

metal coins

sand

mixture

Try this ...

Make your own magnetic slime by mixing liquid glue, food colouring, baking soda and saline solution together with iron filings. Once the slime is ready, hold a magnet above it and move it around. Can you make the slime dance?

In order to find buried treasure, what type of material would it have to be made of?

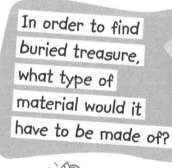

STAGE 2

- Is your mixture from Stage 1 homogeneous or heterogeneous? How do you know?

- Can you separate your mixture using a magnet? Write a hypothesis and then carry out an experiment.

HOW CAN WE SEPARATE SOLIDS FROM LIQUIDS?

Discover...

how to separate components of a mixture using filtration.

Mixtures can be made when one substance is **dissolved** in another. For example, salt dissolves into water to make a salt **solution**.

The substance that dissolves is called the **solute**.

The other substance is the **solvent**.

The particles are completely mixed together.

Can you think of other examples?

solvent

solute

An **insoluble substance** does not dissolve in a solvent. We can use **filtration** to separate these types of mixtures, especially when separating an **insoluble solid** from a **liquid**.

During filtration, we use a **filter** with tiny holes to separate components based on size. A filter can be made of many different materials as long as it allows the solvent to pass through and traps the solute.

The component that stays behind is the **residue**.

The component that passes through the filter is the **filtrate**.

What are these filters used for?

Discuss what is happening with a partner.

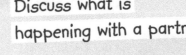

Explore
STAGE 3

- **Why is filtration important for drinking water?**
- **Research different ways to filter dirty water.**
- **Plan and perform an experiment.**

Which organs in our body filter a mixture?

IS THE INK IN A MARKER PEN A PURE SUBSTANCE?

Discover... why chromatography is useful as a type of filtration.

Background: Dissolved colour components can be separated using paper chromatography. When a solution travels through a filter, it carries the dissolved components with it at different rates. Each coloured component will stop at different heights. Paper with coloured spots is called a chromatogram.

Hypothesis: Is ink a pure substance? If so, how many colours should we see?

Materials: coffee filter, scissors, pencil, coloured marker, tape, cup or glass, water, plastic bag

Step 1: Cut the coffee filter into a long strip, 5 cm wide. Draw a line with a coloured marker 3 cm from the bottom. Circle the line in pencil.

Step 2: Fill the cup with 2 cm depth of water. Roll and tape the opposite end of the coffee filter over the pencil, then rest the pencil over the edge of the cup so that the bottom of the filter sits in the water.

Step 3: Place the cup in a plastic bag. Wait a few hours.

Reflect 1 Why should you use pencil?

Reflect 2 How many coloured lines are there? What colours are they?

There were ... coloured lines which means ...

Conclusion: Share your results. Did any markers contain a pure substance?

The ink is / is not a pure substance.

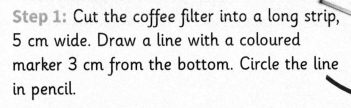

Filtration and paper chromatography are useful in separating insoluble solids from liquids, but what about other solutions?

Evaporation uses heat to separate a **soluble solid** from a **liquid**.

boiling

solution

heat

soluble solid

As the liquid is heated, it evaporates into the air, leaving the solid behind.

What changes of state are evident here?

What is being mined in this photo? How is this formed? Do these exist in Spain?

Look back

In what other ways is evaporation useful to us?

Distillation is a useful method for separating **liquids** from solutions. It is very similar to evaporation, but we use **condensation** to collect the liquid component from its gas state, so that it can be used.

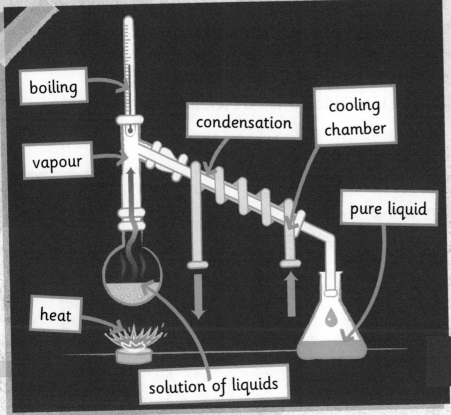

boiling

condensation

cooling chamber

vapour

pure liquid

heat

solution of liquids

It is important to remember that each of the components must boil at different temperatures in order to be separated.

The liquid component that boils at a lower temperature evaporates first, and as a gas, passes through a cooling chamber where it **condenses**.

What remains is a liquid in one container and a pure liquid in another.

Water boils at 100°C, while ethanol boils at 78°C. Describe how to distil a solution of water and ethanol.

How could distillation provide the Earth with clean drinking water?

STAGE 4

- **Plan a distillation experiment to separate the components of apple juice, vinegar and broth.**
- **Which one can you separate the most water from? Write your hypothesis before you begin.**
- **Draw your experiment or ask your teacher to perform the experiment for you.**

… contains the most water.

… does not separate well through distillation because …

1 In your notebook, complete the sentences with the present perfect continuous.

a How long ..... he ..... (work) as a scientist? He ..... (work) in the lab for ten years.

b I am disappointed with the results of my experiment because I ..... (work) very hard on it.

c The beverage ..... (distil) for three months. It will be ready to drink next month.

d Dr Green ..... (study) chromatography since she went to university.

e The water ..... (evaporate) since last Friday when we left the laboratory.

2 Match the sentences.

1 Air completely fills any container.
2 This mixture has a uniform appearance.
3 This substance takes the shape of its container.
4 This metal is attracted to the magnet.
5 There is a substance at the bottom of a solvent.

a It can't be a solid.
b It must be a gas.
c It could be insoluble.
d It must be magnetic.
e It might be homogeneous.

3 🎧 For each question, choose the correct answer.

1 You will hear two classmates talking about an experiment. Which separation method do they decide to use?
   a Filtration
   b Evaporation
   c Distillation

2 You will hear a teacher describing a substance. What state is it in?
   a Solid
   b Liquid
   c Gas

3 You will hear two scientists talking about a mixture. What property has it got?
   a It is homogeneous.
   b It is heterogeneous.
   c They cannot decide.

1 What state are the following mixtures in? Are they homogeneous or heterogeneous? Write sentences.

a

b

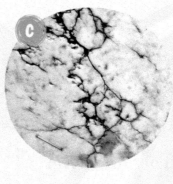
c

d

2

Quiz time

Name the method that ...

a separates an insoluble solid from a liquid.

b separates a soluble solid from a liquid.

c separates a metal from sand.

d separates a soluble solid from a liquid in two separate containers.

e separates two components using a force.

f separates two components using a filter.

g separates a solid using heat.

h separates a liquid using condensation.

For more Unit 4 activities go to page 84.

 FINALE

- Create a poster to show the properties and components of your mixture and the results of the experiments you performed.
- Include pictures, drawings, tables and graphs.
- Discuss your results and conclusions and compare all the different mixtures you have studied.

My conclusions are ...

I found that ...

Using ... to separate this mixture worked better.

Look and discuss...

What chemical reactions are shown in the photos?

Chemical reactions, such as fermentation, oxidation and combustion, occur in nature as well as in the laboratory. Humans have found ways to exploit these chemical changes as well as to prevent them from happening.

In this photo, I think ... is occurring.

It looks like ... is happening.

combustion 1, 6; oxidation 3, 5; fermentation 2, 4

4

Song
Change, change, change

Which of these reactions have you seen? Where?

5

6

DOCUMENTARY
Different reactions

Explore

Write a report about chemical reactions. You will:

- experiment with combustion, oxidation and fermentation.
- learn the value of chemical reactions in our daily lives.
- investigate how to prevent chemical reactions.
- produce a scientific report to create a class magazine.

WHY DO ROTTEN EGGS SMELL SO BAD?

Discover...

the main characteristics of chemical reactions.

During a **chemical reaction**, the atoms within substances are rearranged and joined together in different ways. This results in a substance that is completely different to the original substances.

The original substances are called **reactants** and their **original properties** change as the reaction takes place.

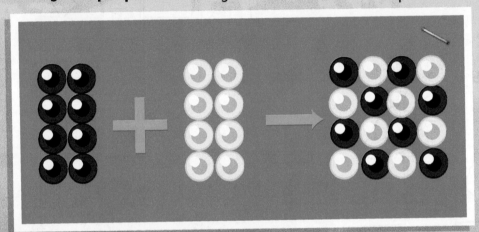

The **new product** formed from a chemical reaction can only be separated again by another chemical reaction because the particles are **chemically linked**. This means simple separation methods, like filtration, evaporation or distillation, won't work.

- What ingredients do you use to make biscuits?
- How do they change after the chemical reaction (when you bake them)?
- What is the product and how is this different from the original ingredients?
- How easy would it be to get the original ingredients back?

How is the product of a chemical reaction different from a mixture?

Thermal energy, oxygen and microorganisms can all cause chemical reactions to take place.

Find out what else can cause chemical reactions.

There are several clues to indicate that a chemical reaction might have taken place. Chemical reactions usually involve a change in appearance or energy.

Energy change

Some chemical reactions either produce or absorb energy. This can be thermal or light energy.

If the products become:

warmer = **exothermic** reaction

colder = **endothermic** reaction

Colour change

When the original reactant changes to make a different coloured product, this is a sign that a chemical reaction has taken place.

Is there a chemical reaction when you mix blue and yellow paint? Explain your answer.

Ice melting into water is not a chemical reaction. Why?

Gas formation

Some chemical reactions produce gas as a product. Bubbles may be produced or you might smell an odour.

When an egg decomposes, the proteins are broken down. Find out what gas is released.

Precipitate formation

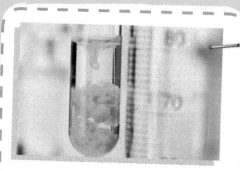

A precipitate is a solid that forms when two solutions are combined. It is a very common sign of a chemical reaction because it shows a change in composition.

Explore   STAGE 1

- **Find out about other chemical reactions. Can you reproduce any at home?**
- **With a partner, discuss the characteristics that prove each one is a chemical reaction.**

What happens when you dip a copper coin into a solution of white vinegar and salt? Can you explain why?

HOW DOES A FIRE KEEP BURNING?

Combustion (or burning) is a rapid chemical combination of a substance with oxygen. Energy is produced in the form of **light** and **heat**. It also produces new substances, like **smoke** and **ash**.

In order for something to burn, there must be **oxygen**, **fuel** and **energy**. If one side of the fire triangle is removed, the **fire** will go out.

How could this information help firefighters tackle different fires?

Air is about 21% **oxygen**. When oxygen from the atmosphere reacts with fuel, combustion occurs.

Heat or thermal **energy** must be added for combustion to take place.

What makes up the other 79% of air?

Fuel is anything that burns, including wood, gas and oil.

OXYGEN · HEAT · FUEL

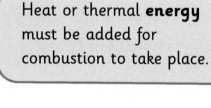 **Explore** STAGE 2

- Research and discuss the positive and negative effects of combustion.
- How can we use our knowledge of combustion to prevent fires at home, school and in nature?
- Draw a chart in your notebook and record the information.

 **Look back**

Is combustion an exothermic or endothermic chemical reaction?

Chemical reaction	Advantages	Disadvantages	Prevention

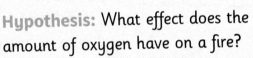

HOW DOES THE AMOUNT OF OXYGEN AFFECT A FIRE?

Find Out more...

Discover...

the role oxygen plays in combustion.

Background: Combustion is a chemical reaction that requires oxygen. If there is not enough oxygen, a fire cannot continue to burn.

Hypothesis: What effect does the amount of oxygen have on a fire?

Materials: three glass jars of different sizes, four identical candles in holders, lighter or matches, timer

This experiment requires the use of fire. Review the laboratory safety tips on page 85 before starting.

Step 1: Work with a partner. Prepare the timer and carefully light all the candles.

Step 2: Cover each candle, except one, with a jar. Begin timing. Observe and record the time that each candle burns out.

Conclusion: Do all the candles burn for the same amount of time? Why or why not? What happens to the oxygen inside the jars?

Reflect 1

Why are all the jars different sizes? Why is there one candle without a jar?

The candle in the ... jar burns for the longest / shortest time because ...

As the chemical reaction takes place, oxygen ...

Why would closing windows and doors help to prevent a fire from spreading quickly in a burning building?

WHY DO BANANAS TURN BLACK?

Discover...

the problems oxidation can cause.

Oxidation is a chemical reaction where a substance changes because **oxygen** is added.

We can see oxidation occurring in different foods and on metals. The atoms of these substances react with oxygen in the air to make new substances, which are normally a different colour.

What's the matter with you?

Too much oxygen!

When some metals, like iron, react with oxygen and **water**, they go rusty. **Rust** is a reddish-brown substance that easily breaks apart and usually makes the original object useless.

Although salt does not cause oxidation, it does speed it up!

Find out other ways to speed up rusting.

Oxidation also occurs in food. When oxygen comes into contact with the chemicals in food, the food begins to discolour and break down. If this continues, the food will lose its nutritional value.

What natural defences protect food from oxidation?

Explore
STAGE 3

- **How can we prevent oxidation? Perform some simple experiments on food to find out!**
- **Research ways to prevent metal from rusting.**
- **In what circumstances is oxidation useful?**
- **Add the information to your chart.**

Oxidation can be prevented by ...

Try this ...

Give a banana a tattoo! Draw a design on tracing paper, then lay it over a banana. With a needle, poke the skin of the banana, following your design. Wait a few minutes. What happens? Why?

WHY DOES PIZZA DOUGH RISE?

Discover...

how we use fermentation to make different products.

Fermentation is a natural, necessary and useful chemical reaction. It occurs when there is no oxygen and involves **microorganisms** which transform **sugars** into organic substances.

Find a fermented product hidden in the unit.

Look at the photos. How is fermentation useful?

Try making yoghurt or cheese at home. Find a recipe online.

Different microorganisms produce different products during the chemical reaction:

Bacteria produce **lactic acid** and **carbon dioxide**.

Try this ...

Fill three bottles with warm water. Add yeast to the first, sugar to the second and both yeast and sugar to the third. Place a balloon over each bottle and wait for an hour. What happens? Why?

Can you think of any other ways we use fermentation?

Explore — STAGE 4

- Fermentation is often used for food preservation. Find out how and why.
- Which foods can be fermented? Are there any disadvantages?
- Can fermentation be prevented?
- Add the information to your chart.

To prevent ... we ferment certain foods.

Fermentation can be used to ...

1 Complete the sentences in your notebook. Use the example to help you.

a Fungi and bacteria cannot make food *themselves*. Instead, they must break down other living beings through fermentation.

b When energy is added in the presence of oxygen and fuel, a fire will start ..... .

c My mother is learning to make yoghurt ..... by fermenting cream.

d Old metal tools left out in the rain will start to oxidise and rust by ..... .

e Pizza dough rises all by ..... because it contains yeast.

2 🎧 You will hear three short conversations. There is one question for each conversation. For each question, choose the correct photo. Which type of chemical reaction is taking place?

1

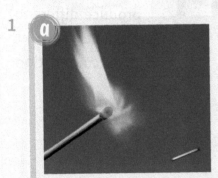

2

3

Content Review

1 Has a chemical reaction taken place in each photo? Explain your answer.

a

b

c

d

2 Work with a partner. Take turns asking and answering the following questions.

a Which chemical reaction was the most interesting to learn about? Why?

b What would you do if you saw a fire?

c Why is it important to save energy that is produced by combustion?

d How can you prevent oxidation? Discuss the different ways.

e Do you think it is important to preserve food using fermentation? Who might benefit from this?

Assessment link

For more Unit 5 activities go to page 86.

 Explore

FINALE

- Prepare a written report about combustion, oxidation or fermentation. You can choose to focus on one, or compare all three.

- Remember to begin with an introduction and end with an interesting conclusion.

  ... is useful because ...

- Share your article with other classmates in a small group.

- Your teacher will combine all the articles into a science magazine for the class to enjoy.

  It is important to prevent ... because ...

6 MAGNETISM

It seems like magic when we open a car door with a remote control or hear a doorbell ring. These devices, along with many others, simply take advantage of the interaction between electricity and magnetism.

Look and discuss...

How are magnets used in these devices?

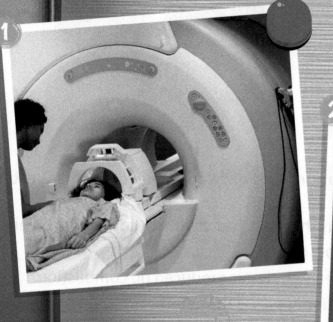

1

2

3

CREDIT CARD

1234 5678 1234 5678

MONTH/YEAR
VALID 05/12   EXPIRES 10/15
FROM

CARDHOLDER NAME

Without magnets, we wouldn't be able to ...

1 to see inside the body; 2 to attach objects to a surface; 3 to encode information; 4 to show direction; 5 to move; 6 to lock; 7 to move; 8 to complete an electric circuit

Magnets allow us to ...

S ng
Attracted to you

In what other ways do we use magnets?

D▶CUMENTARY
It's all about the field

Explore

Create an experiment for a science fair. You will:

- learn about and experiment with magnets.
- use the Earth's magnetism to your advantage.
- understand magnetism and its connection to electricity.
- test a hypothesis, record the results and develop a conclusion.

WHAT IS A MAGNET?

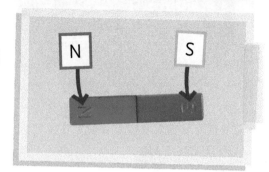

Magnets are used in lots of places, but what are they?

A magnet is any object which has a **magnetic force**. This means it can attract certain metals, like iron. This attraction is called **magnetism**.

A **permanent magnet** always has a magnetic force which cannot be turned off. Permanent magnets can be **man-made** from magnetic materials.

An **induced magnet** or temporary magnet only gives off a magnetic force for a period of time. Although some metals might appear to be magnets, they may simply be temporarily **magnetised**.

Can you name some permanent magnets?

Try this...

Make an induced magnet by rubbing one metal paper clip with the end of a magnet 30 times. Place it close to another paper clip. What happens? Why?

Some **natural magnets** are found in nature, like the mineral **magnetite**.

Explore   STAGE 1

- Are most materials magnetic or non-magnetic? Discuss with a partner and do some research.
- How are the magnetic materials useful?
- Create a spider diagram to organise this information.

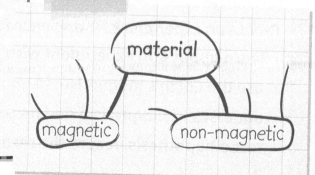

material

magnetic   non-magnetic

HOW DOES A MAGNET HOLD UP A PIECE OF PAPER ON A FRIDGE?

Discover...

what a magnetic field is.

Magnets have long confused scientists because the magnetic force can act on objects that do not touch. Scientists use the idea of a **magnetic field** to explain this.

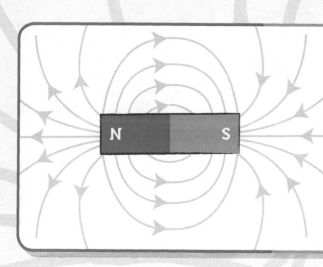

Although it is normally invisible, a magnetic field is the area that fills a space where a magnetic force works. It is produced by moving charges.

If you hold a magnet in one hand and a paper clip in the other, what do you feel when you bring them closer? Why?

You can observe a magnetic field if you lay **iron** filings on a surface and place a magnet in the middle. The filings will arrange themselves in **field lines**.

As charges move more, how might a magnetic field's strength change?

Every magnet creates its own magnetic field, which affects neighbouring objects. The force can also pass through non-magnetic objects, like paper or plastic. However, not all magnets are the same strength.

Can magnetic forces overcome gravity? Think of examples.

WHY CAN'T YOU PUSH SOME MAGNETS TOGETHER?

No matter how hard you try, sometimes you cannot push two magnets together. Try it yourself!

Discover...

the main forces at work within a magnet and their effects on materials.

In all magnetic objects, the moving charges begin and end at **magnetic poles**. Magnets have two poles: a **north pole** (N) and a **south pole** (S). The poles are where the magnetism is strongest.

If you put any two magnets together, there are two things that can happen:

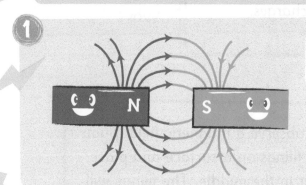

1 Each pole is attracted to a pole with the opposite charge.

The magnets come together because the opposite poles **attract** each other.

2

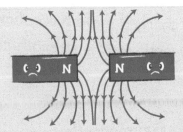

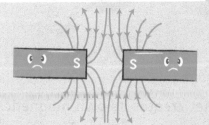

The magnets push each other away because identical poles **repel** each other.

Place non-magnetised iron next to a bar magnet. What happens when you touch each end of the magnet to the metal? Now try the same with magnetised iron. What happens now?

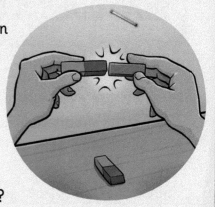

We have learnt that magnets can be temporary or permanent, but how can we distinguish a true magnet from a magnetic material?

Just because an object is attracted to a magnet does not mean that it is a magnet itself. Magnets are identified by their ability to repel another known magnet.

Gold and silver are not magnetic.

How can we use magnets to spot fake jewellery?

Explore — STAGE 2

- Are magnetic fields affected by all materials equally? Work with a partner to plan an experiment. What materials will you need? Make sure you include plastic, wood and different metals.

- Carry out your experiment, then test the following: What happens if you place thin objects between the two magnets? How thick can an object be before it affects the magnetic field?

I think ... because ...

- Make sure you record your hypotheses, results and conclusions in an organised way.

The results show that ...

HOW DOES A COMPASS WORK?

Discover...

the Earth's magnetic field.

Magnets are everywhere, even under our feet! The Earth's magnetic field protects us and can also be used to help us if we get lost.

Since the core of our planet is filled with hot, liquid iron, the Earth has a huge magnetic field.

Just like on a bar magnet, the Earth's poles are where the field lines come together. We call them the **North Pole** and the **South Pole**.

Find out what the difference is between the *magnetic poles* and the *geographical poles*.

magnetic field

magnetic North Pole

geographical North Pole

iron core

geographical South Pole

magnetic South Pole

The magnetic field acts like the Earth's sunglasses. It protects our atmosphere by deflecting harmful UV rays from the sun as well as space radiation and particles from **solar wind**.

Find out more about solar wind. What is it?

What part does the Earth's magnetic field play in the *Aurora Borealis* and *Aurora Australis*? Where and when can you see these?

We can use the Earth's magnetic field to our advantage!

A **compass** is a navigational instrument that uses a magnetised needle. The cardinal points **north**, **south**, **east** and **west** are marked on the inner circle, or the **compass rose**, surrounding the needle. The degrees are also marked.

Since a compass always points towards the **Earth's magnetic North Pole**, all you have to do is line the compass needle up with the N of the rose, and you know you are facing north.

Many living things, like bees, pigeons and salmon, can detect the Earth's magnetic field and use it to navigate. You could say they have an inner compass!

Find one of these animals hidden in the unit.

Hold a compass in your hand, facing north. Where are west, east and south? Try facing a different direction.

Using a compass and a map to navigate has become a sport called orienteering.

Find out how to do this, then practise with a friend! Make your own map and plan a treasure hunt for your classmates.

Explore STAGE 3

- **Build your own compass using a dish of water, a needle, a magnet and half a cork.**
- **Magnetise the needle by rubbing it with the magnet.**
- **Work out how to arrange the water, needle and cork. Experiment with different designs.**
- **Test your design against a real compass.**

CAN YOU SWITCH A MAGNET ON AND OFF?

Discover...
the relationship between electricity and magnetism.

Anywhere there is magnetism, you will find **electricity** nearby.

What are the other parts of an atom?

All matter is made up of atoms. The negatively charged electrons move around the outside of each atom. If the electrons all move in the same direction, like in magnetic materials, a tiny magnetic field is produced. However, in most materials, electrons move in different directions so the magnetism is cancelled.

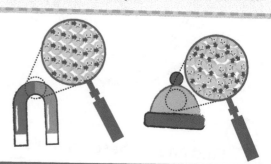

In an **electric current**, the electrons moving through a wire create a magnetic field. When placed close together, two wires with flowing current will attract or repel like two magnets.

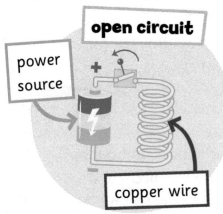

open circuit

power source

copper wire

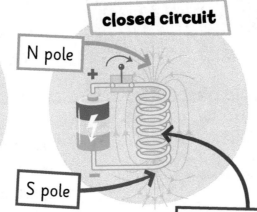

closed circuit

N pole

S pole

electromagnet

Using electricity, we can create a magnetic field by forcing electrons to move in the same direction. This is called an **electromagnet**. It acts like a magnet, but only when an electric current flows through it.

🎧 Listen to the programme about electromagnetism. Write the names of the scientists and their contributions.

Electromagnets are useful because they can be turned on and off. Many everyday objects contain electromagnets.

Research the uses of electromagnets.

STAGE 4

- **How might a magnet interfere with a mobile phone, a stereo or a credit card?**
- **Find out by performing the Ørsted experiment. Use a compass and an electric current. What does this show?**

HOW CAN YOU MAKE AN ELECTROMAGNET STRONGER?

Discover... the relationship between electricity and magnetism through experimentation.

Background: An electromagnet uses an electrical current to create a magnetic field. Changes in the electric current result in changes in the strength of the electromagnet. Develop your own experiment to test this.

Hypothesis: How can you make an electromagnet stronger?

Materials: copper wire, two or more batteries, iron nail or screw, paper clips, fork

You could try one of the following: wrapping more coils around the iron core, increasing the current, turning the battery around.

Step 1: Build a circuit using the battery and copper wire. Wrap the wire loosely around the iron nail to create coils. Test the electromagnet on the paper clips and fork.

Step 2: Experiment with different options and test the strength of the magnet each time. For each change you make, record the results.

Reflect①
How does each end of the nail react?

Reflect②
How many paper clips can the electromagnet lift? Can it lift the fork?

Reflect③
For each option, how many paper clips were lifted? Could it lift the fork?

Conclusion: What changes made the electromagnet stronger?

By ... , we can make an electromagnet stronger.

Making an electromagnet stronger means ...

Why are extremely strong electromagnets useful? Where do we use them?

25 pts.

1 **Complete the sentences in your notebook. Use the example to help you.**

a If the needle on a compass *reads* south, you *will have* to turn around to go north.

b If two opposite poles ..... (be) placed nearby, they ..... (attract), and the magnets ..... (come) together.

c The magnetic field ..... (increase) if the electrical charge ..... (increase).

d A mobile phone ..... (not work) if you ..... (place) it near a magnet.

e If you ..... (bring) two like poles together, the magnets ..... (push) each other away because they repel.

2 **Read the email from your friend, Daniel, and the notes you have made. Write a reply. Write about 100 words.**

To:

From: Daniel

Hi,

My science class is learning about magnets right now. Do you know anything about them? —— Lots – say what

I would love to plan an experiment. Would you like to help me? —— Great!

We could meet up this weekend, if you're not too busy. Afterwards, we could do something more relaxing.

Talk to you soon,

Daniel

Say which day; Suggest an activity

1 Complete the sentences using words from the box.

> magnet   magnetic   magnetise   magnetism   magnetite

a ..... is an object's ability to attract certain metals.

b It is possible to ..... a metal and make a temporary magnet by running an electric current through it.

c The mineral ..... is a natural magnet.

d A ..... is any piece of metal that has a magnetic force.

e Iron, cobalt and nickel are all ..... metals that can be used to make permanent magnets.

2 How are these photos related? Talk with a partner.

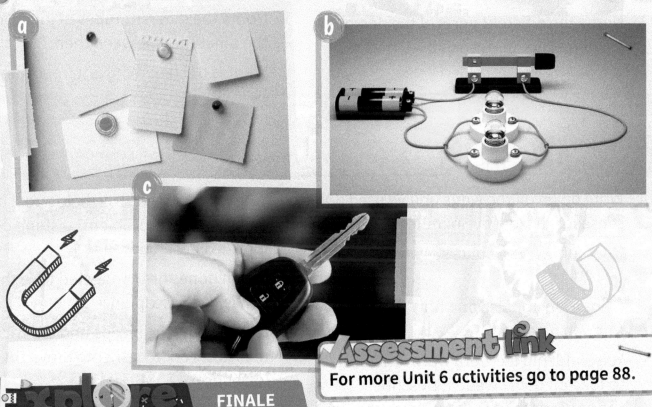

Assessment link

For more Unit 6 activities go to page 88.

Explore   FINALE

- Based on one of the experiments from the unit, choose one to demonstrate at a science fair.

- Prepare a poster. What information should you include?

- Set up your experiment.

- Be prepared to explain and demonstrate your experiment many times!

My hypothesis is ...

As you can see, ... happens when ...

So, my conclusion is ...

(1) Questions

Think about it

1. Name the five main sense organs. What is each one sensitive to?

2. Describe how a stimulus received from each of the five senses reaches our brain.

3. What is a neuron?

4. Name and describe the three different types of neuron.

5. Name the different parts of the nervous system. What does each part include?

6. Which part of the brain is responsible for the following actions: a balance? b thinking? c involuntary actions?

7. How many bones can you name? Where are they?

8. What do skeletal, cardiac and smooth muscle do? How?

9. Name the different types of joint. What is the difference between them?

10. What is a reflex? Why is it important?

Think harder

1. Write down all the ways you've used your senses in the last five minutes.

2. How can we see a blue sweater in front of us?

3. What is an impulse and how does it travel through a neuron?

4. You suddenly feel very warm and decide to take off your sweater. Describe the nerve pathway along which the impulse travels.

5. Which part of the nervous system is responsible for reflexes? Describe the pathway.

6. Which part of the brain helps you: a solve a mathematics problem? b stand on one foot? c digest food?

7. Which bones are connected to: a the pelvis? b the scapula?

8. Explain how the biceps and the triceps muscles work together to move the lower arm.

9. In a yoga class, everyone is asked to touch their toes. How can they do this?

10. As you are walking, you step on a sharp object. What happens next? Why?

Study aid

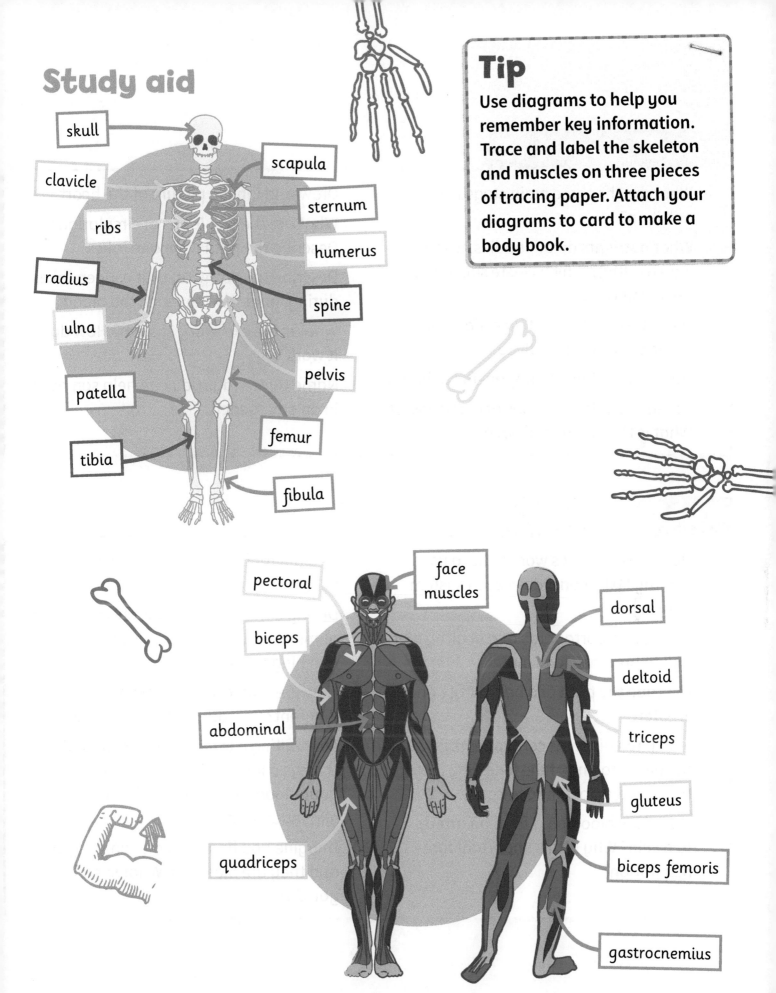

skull

clavicle

ribs

radius

ulna

patella

tibia

scapula

sternum

humerus

spine

pelvis

femur

fibula

Tip

Use diagrams to help you remember key information. Trace and label the skeleton and muscles on three pieces of tracing paper. Attach your diagrams to card to make a body book.

pectoral

biceps

abdominal

quadriceps

face muscles

dorsal

deltoid

triceps

gluteus

biceps femoris

gastrocnemius

2 Questions

1 What are the three main stages of human nutrition?

2 What nutrients do our bodies need to stay healthy? Which waste substances are eliminated?

3 Describe the stages of digestion and name the organs involved.

4 Name the different components of blood.

5 Name the different types of blood vessel. What is the function of each?

6 Draw and label a picture of the heart.

7 What are the two loops of circulation? Describe the path each one takes.

8 Describe the pathway that oxygen takes during inhalation to reach the blood.

9 What is the excretory system? How does it work?

10 Name three ways you can help someone in an emergency.

Think harder

1 How do our bodies work to keep us healthy? What part does each system play in this?

2 Why is it important to eat a healthy diet and to breathe clean air?

3 Describe the path of a hamburger once it is eaten.

4 Match the different components in the blood to one of the following jobs: transporter, doctor, repairman.

5 How does blood pass from an artery to a vein? Why is this important for respiration?

6 As a doctor listens to your heart, they will hear two sounds. Why?

7 During a heart attack, your heart cannot pump blood. How does this affect oxygen reaching the brain?

8 How are inhalation and exhalation different? Compare the two processes.

9 After eating a large meal of fast food, there is a lot of waste flowing through your blood. How does the body eliminate waste?

10 Imagine you find someone on the ground and they are bleeding. What should you do?

Study aid

Tip
Add to your body book by drawing each system on tracing paper and labelling the organs. Use the information below to help you.

Digestive system

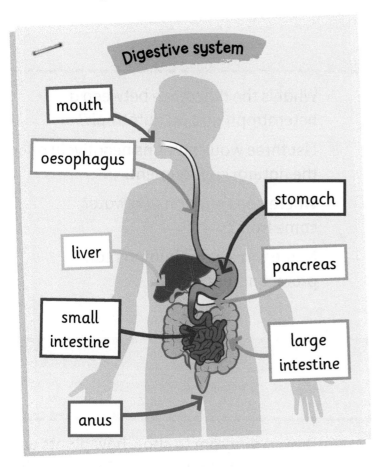

- mouth
- oesophagus
- liver
- small intestine
- anus
- stomach
- pancreas
- large intestine

Circulatory system

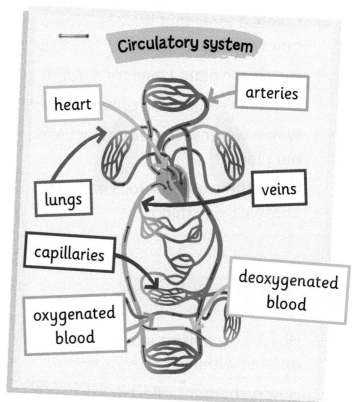

- heart
- lungs
- capillaries
- oxygenated blood
- arteries
- veins
- deoxygenated blood

Respiratory system

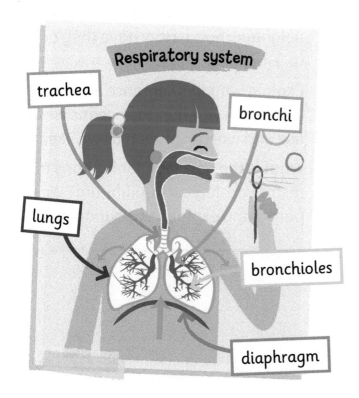

- trachea
- lungs
- bronchi
- bronchioles
- diaphragm

Excretory system

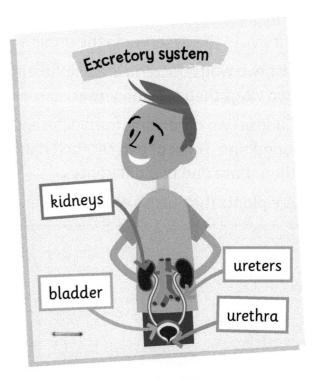

- kidneys
- bladder
- ureters
- urethra

(3) Questions

Think about it

1. How do we classify living things?
2. Create a table that lists the five kingdoms and describes their characteristics.
3. How is the plant kingdom divided?
4. List three ways living things use water?
5. Why is water so important for life on our planet?
6. Name three objects you can use to observe living things.
7. What is the difference between a heterotroph and an autotroph?
8. List three ways humans negatively affect the natural environment.
9. Where does our drinking water come from?
10. Name three ways humans can protect nature.

Think harder

1. How do organisms interact with one another within an ecosystem?
2. How do humans affect organisms from each of the five kingdoms?
3. Can organisms from the Monera kingdom survive in the desert or in the arctic?
4. List two ways bacteria are helpful and two ways they are dangerous.
5. Choose two organisms from different kingdoms. Think of two characteristics they share and two differences.
6. Are plants the Earth's only producers?
7. Draw a diagram to show how plants use water for photosynthesis. Then, describe the steps.
8. Name five living things that live in your neighbourhood. How have they adapted to living near humans?
9. Explain why this sentence is false: There is so much water in the oceans we can use and waste as much as we like.
10. What is the best way for humans to restore ecological equilibrium? Write a paragraph explaining your opinion.

Study aid

Tip
Cluster maps can help you learn and practise new words. Make your own to study vocabulary from Unit 3.

Word:

Synonym:

Antonym:

Definition:

Draw a picture:

Use it in a sentence:

Word:
sustainable

Synonym:
renewable

Antonym:
unsustainable

Definition: causing very little or no damage to the environment and so able to continue for a long time

Draw a picture:

Use it in a sentence:
The forestry company made sure the number of trees cut down was <u>sustainable</u>.

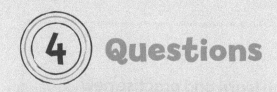

4 Questions

Think about it

1 What is a mixture? Give three examples.

2 What are the different states of matter? Give an example of each.

3 Give an example of a pure substance and describe it.

4 Explain the difference between homogeneous and heterogeneous mixtures.

5 What type of components can we separate using magnetism? Give some examples.

6 What is a solution? What are its components called? Give some examples.

7 What is the difference between a soluble and an insoluble solid? Write a definition for each.

8 How can we use evaporation to separate components in a mixture?

9 How do evaporation and distillation differ? When should each method be used?

10 Explain the steps of distillation to a partner. Use a diagram to help.

Think harder

1 Are the components of a mixture organised? Explain your answer.

2 Can a substance change states? If so, what is necessary to make this change?

3 Can a gas be a mixture? If so, give an example.

4 Think about chocolate milk. Is it a pure substance? Is it homogeneous or heterogeneous? Describe the components.

5 While you are playing in a pile of leaves, your friend's keys fall out of his pocket. Devise a plan to help him find his keys.

6 How can scientists at a water treatment facility use charcoal, gravel, rocks and sand to filter drinking water? In what order would you arrange these objects? Why?

7 Which methods of separation can be used in the kitchen? Give examples.

8 Is it possible to separate rocks, salt and sand from the beach? If so, how?

9 How does our body use evaporation?

10 When using distillation, why is it important for the components to boil at different temperatures?

Study aid

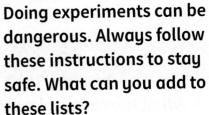

Tip

Doing experiments can be dangerous. Always follow these instructions to stay safe. What can you add to these lists?

✗ Don't

- Taste, eat, drink or inhale anything unless you are told to by the teacher.
- Play with materials or equipment.
- Mess around with your friends.
- Run around.

✓ Do

- Stay safe and behave responsibly.
- Wash your hands.
- Tie long hair back.
- Follow instructions carefully.
- Be careful with sharp tools. Always cut material away from yourself and others.
- Keep your hands away from your face, eyes and mouth during experiments.
- Use heat-resistant gloves to touch hot objects.
- Ignite matches and lighters away from your body and other people.

Matches and lighters are not toys. Use them carefully and always with an adult.

5 Questions

Think about it

1 What is a chemical reaction? Write a definition and give three examples.

2 How do the products of a chemical reaction differ from a mixture?

3 What can cause chemical reactions to occur?

4 What are the four clues that indicate a chemical reaction may have taken place?

5 Can you undo chemical changes easily? Explain your answer.

6 Name the three things that are required for something to burn.

7 What are the products of combustion?

8 For oxidation to occur, what element must be present?

9 What is fermentation? What living things are involved?

10 Why is fermentation useful?

Think harder

1 Describe what happens during a chemical reaction. Draw an illustration.

2 Describe the difference between *a* and *b*:

   a The mirror in the bathroom is covered with condensation after a hot shower.

   b You light a candle on a birthday cake.

3 In these examples, what is the cause of each chemical reaction?

   a In an apple, sugar is transformed into lactic acid and carbon dioxide.

   b A cut apple left out on the counter turns brown.

   c An apple pie is baking in an oven.

4 Name three chemical changes that take place inside human beings.

5 A scientist mixes two clear solutions together. There is a terrible smell and a blue solid forms that emits light. What indicates a chemical reaction has taken place? What could you do to be certain?

6 How is combustion a chemical change?

7 What are the differences between oxidation and combustion? Are they both useful? Why?

8 How is rust formed? Is it possible to speed up this reaction?

9 Can fermentation take place when oxygen is present? Explain.

10 Give an example of oxidation, fermentation and combustion. Explain what happens in each case.

Study aid

Tip
Use a table to summarise key information. Complete this table about chemical reactions in your notebook.

Chemical reaction	Reactants	Products	Cause
Combustion	oxygen, fuel, energy	light and heat energy, smoke, ash	rapid thermal energy increase
Oxidation			
Fermentation			

6 Questions

Think about it

1 What is a magnet? Describe its properties and characteristics.

2 List five uses of magnets.

3 Make a Venn diagram comparing permanent and temporary magnets.

4 What is a magnetic field?

5 Draw the magnetic field lines of two magnets whose north and south poles are touching.

6 Explain how the poles of a magnet work.

7 Draw a diagram showing Earth's magnetic poles. Explain why they are important for us on Earth?

8 How does a compass work? Discuss with a partner.

9 What is an electromagnet?

10 Name three electric devices that use magnets.

Think harder

1 Can we find magnets in nature? Give examples.

2 Your friend rubs a key with a magnet over and over again. When he touches the metal doorknob, his key sticks to it. Explain what has happened.

3 A magnet can hold a non-magnetic object on a metal surface. How is this possible?

4 If a magnet is attracted to another magnet, do they have similar or opposite charged poles?

5 A temporary magnet will attract a drawing pin, but not a gold necklace. Why?

6 Are magnetic north and geographical north the same thing? Explain your answer.

7 Is a compass always correct? How could you interfere with a compass reading?

8 How are electricity and magnetism similar?

9 Have electromagnets got permanent magnetic properties? Explain.

10 Predict which of the following will be attracted to an electromagnet: iron fork, wooden spoon, metal paperclip, silver ring. Explain your answers.

Study aid

Tip
This concept map shows the relationship between magnetism and electricity. Complete the concept map in your notebook. How could you add to it?

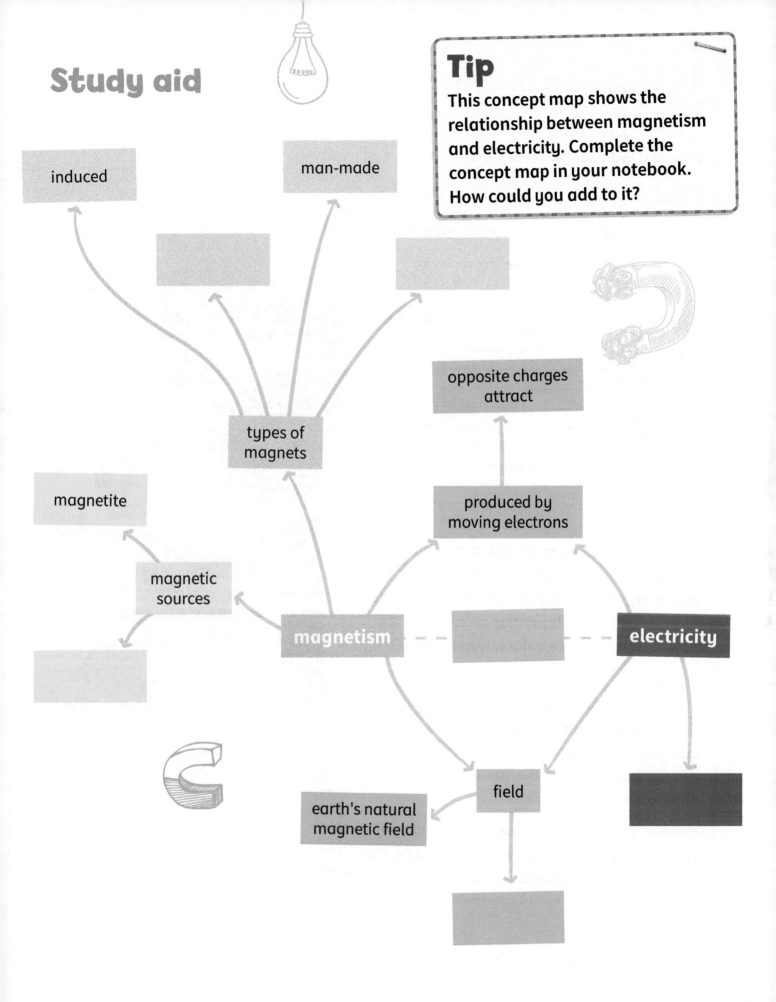

induced

man-made

opposite charges attract

produced by moving electrons

types of magnets

magnetite

magnetic sources

magnetism

electricity

field

earth's natural magnetic field

1 Get on my nerves

Experiment with sensory receptors.

Materials: ruler, three toothpicks, eraser

Step 1: Copy and complete the chart to record your results.

Test		Fingertip	Forearm	Shoulder
1	Stimulus			
	Response			
2	Stimulus			
	Response			
3	Stimulus			
	Response			
4	Stimulus			
	Response			
5	Stimulus			
	Response			

Step 2: Work in pairs. Create a stimulus probe by sticking one toothpick into one side of an eraser, and two toothpicks into the other side, 3 cm apart. You will use this to compare the stimulus you give with the response felt by your partner.

Step 3: Take turns to close your eyes while the stimulus probe is used to test whether you feel one or two touches on different parts of your body. Record the stimulus and the response for each touch.

Step 4: Repeat the test five times in each of the three different body areas, alternating the stimulus probe randomly.

Why do you think some parts of the body are more sensitive than others? (Hint: A sensory nerve can only send one signal at a time.)

Why is it important for different parts of the body to be more sensitive than others?

② System models

Choose a system and make a three-dimensional model using recycled materials.

Materials: large poster board, pencil, scissors, glue, colouring materials, recycled materials

Step 1: Choose one of the systems covered in the unit. Trace a basic outline of the system on your poster board and include all the organs.

Step 2: Think about the shape, size, texture and function of each organ. Choose recycled materials that best represent each one and build a 3D model.

Step 3: Label your model and explain how the system works to a friend or family member.

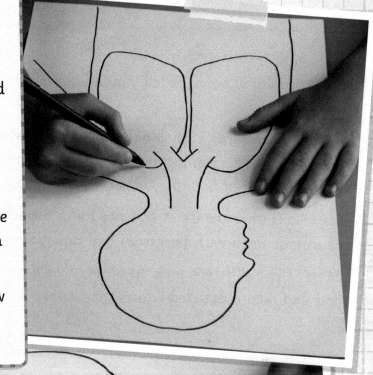

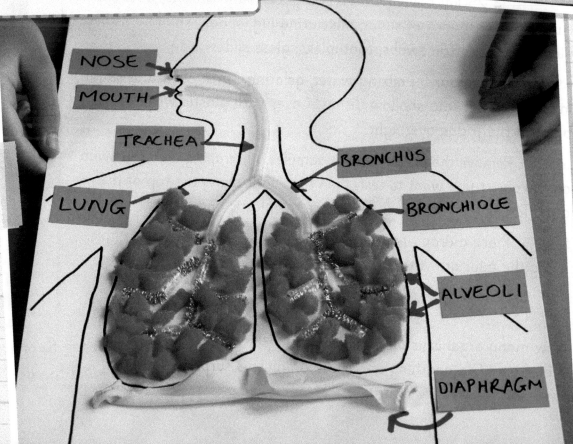

NOSE
MOUTH
TRACHEA
LUNG
BRONCHUS
BRONCHIOLE
ALVEOLI
DIAPHRAGM

③ Studying life

Life is all around us, and if you take the time to look more carefully, it can surprise you! You can view organisms from the five kingdoms in a number of ways. If you observe them in their natural habitat, you are studying them **in the field**. However, you can also study them more closely **in the laboratory**. We use different instruments in each place.

Part A: Working in the field

Materials: notebook, pencil, magnifying glass, binoculars, glass jar, ruler

Step 1: Transform a small notebook into a field journal by copying and filling in this information: *date and time, location, weather, type of habitat, fun or interesting observations, sketches.*

Step 2: Gather the items you need into a backpack. Visit an area near your town with terrestrial and aquatic ecosystems.

Step 3: Use different tools to observe each new organism you find and record detailed information about it.

Part B: Working in the lab

Materials: 250ml boiling water, two packets of gelatine, beef stock cube, two teaspoons of sugar, measuring jug, spoon, shallow dishes, plastic wrap, cotton swabs, toothpicks, glass slides

Step 1: Make agar by mixing water, gelatine, stock cube and sugar in a bowl. Pour into shallow dishes. Cover with plastic wrap and place in the fridge overnight.

Step 2: Remove the plastic. Collect samples by scraping a cotton swab on the object you want to test, then running it along the top of the agar. Test one object per dish. Replace the plastic and allow to grow.

Step 3: Place a drop of water on to a glass slide. Scrape a toothpick along the agar growth and mix it in the drop of water. Observe the slide under a microscope and take notes. Repeat for other plates.

Conclusions:

How many organisms did you observe? Which kingdoms were they from? Did anything about the organisms surprise you?

Be very careful not to disturb an organism's habitat! Always return organisms to where you found them!

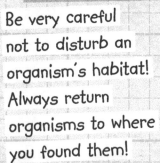

Trace the microscope and label the parts. Find out what each part does.

Super sweet solutions

Mix a super saturated solution and use it to make rock candy.

Why should you heat the water?

Materials: wooden skewer, clothes peg, narrow glass jar, ¼ measuring cup, one cup of water, two cups of sugar, food colouring

Step 1: Heat the water until it boils and add it to the jar.

Step 2: Add ¼ cup of sugar to the water and stir until the sugar has completely dissolved.

Step 3: Continue adding sugar to the solution in small amounts and stir. Continue until no more sugar will dissolve.

Step 4: Allow the solution to cool for about 10 minutes and place the skewer in the mixture using the clothes peg to hold it in place.

Step 5: Add food colouring to the solution and place it somewhere safe.

Step 6: Check daily and watch the crystals grow. In 3–7 days, you will be able to eat your candy!

Why do you think the sugar crystals form on the skewer?

5 Shedding light on combustion

Experiment with combustion and water.

Materials: candle, plate, glass jar, glass of cold water, food colouring

Step 1: Add food colouring to the water, then pour a thin layer on to the plate.

Step 2: Place the candle in the centre of the plate and light it.

Step 3: Before you cover the candle with the jar, write a hypothesis saying what you think will happen.

Step 4: Quickly and carefully place the jar over the top of the candle.

Observations: What happens to the flame? Why? What happens to the water? Research why this happens.

(6) Electromagnetic machine

Build an electromagnetic motor using household materials. You can use this motor to do work if you like.

Materials: plasticine, battery, two paper clips, electrical tape, copper wire, sandpaper, magnets

Step 1: Form a pad of plasticine and place the battery on top.

Step 2: Straighten out each paper clip, then bend one end to form a loop. Attach one paper clip to each pole of the battery with electrical tape.

Step 3: Coil the copper wire many times to form a circle the size of a large coin, leaving out the two ends. Rub each end with sandpaper to remove the copper. Feed each end through the paper clip loop so the copper circle sits between the two clips above the battery.

Step 4: Place the magnet on top of the battery, under the copper circle. What happens?

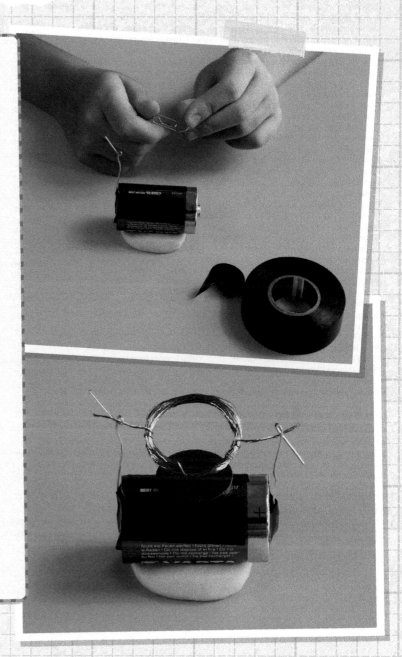

If the copper wire does not start spinning right away, try rotating it with your finger to get it started.

How could you use this motor to power a toy car made out of recycled materials?

CAMBRIDGE
UNIVERSITY PRESS

Acknowledgements

The authors and publishers acknowledge the following sources of copyright material and are grateful for the permissions granted. While every effort has been made, it has not always been possible to identify the sources of all the material used, or to trace all copyright holders. If any omissions are brought to our notice, we will be happy to include the appropriate acknowledgements on reprinting and in the next update to the digital edition, as applicable.

Key: FM = First Matter, U = Unit.

Photo acknowledgements

All the photographs are sourced from Getty Images.

FM: RASimon/iStock/Getty Images Plus; **U0:** Bettmann; Donaldson Collection/Michael Ochs Archives; Donaldson Collection/Michael Ochs Archives; Keystone Features/Hulton Archive; ZU_09/DigitalVision Vectors; **U1:** Jupiterimages/Photolibrary; Fabrice Lerouge/ONOKY; mira/Moment; thehague/iStock Editorial/Getty Images plus; Muhammad Danial Mohd Fauzi/EyeEm Premium; tillsonburg/E+; Image Source; ArtMassa/iStock/Getty Images Plus; Lesley Wang; Thomas Odulate/Cultura; PhotoAlto/Michele Constantini PhotoAlto Agency; fizkes/iStock/Getty Images Plus; Ljupco/iStock/Getty Images Plus; adamkaz/iStock/Getty Images Plus; Russell Burden/Photolibrary/Getty Images Plus; Hailshadow/iStock/Getty Images Plus; Aurelien Meunier/Getty Images Sport; Sidekick/E+; Pitton/iStock/Getty Images Plus; Sebastian Kaulitzki/Science Photo Library; jaminwell/E+; Juan Diaz/EyeEm; Spauln/E+; James Lang/EyeEm; **U2:** Ian Hooton/Science Photo Library; simonkr/E+; H.Klosowska/Moment; Westend61; James Darell/Cultura; Image Source; bbbrrn/iStock/Getty Images Plus; laindiapiaroa; fstop123/E+; Photo_Concepts/Cultura; Tetra images; Andy Crawford/Dorling Kindersley/Getty Images Plus; Igphotography/iStock/Getty Images Plus; Bonilla1879/iStock/Getty Images Plus; turk_stock_photographer/iStock/Getty Images Plus; Zocha_K/E+; Fotosearch; Sawitree Pamee/EyeEm; Stockbyte; Gary Ombler/Dorling Kindersley/Getty Images Plus; Mike Kemp; fcafotodigital/E+; natapetrovich/iStock/Getty Images Plus; Leonard Gertz/Corbis/Getty Images Plus; Maskot; **U3:** shan.shihan/Moment; Elva Etienne/Moment; Johner Images; Peter Zelei images/MomentHakan Jansson/Maskot; Monty Rakusen/Cultura; Alex E. Proimos/Moment; Miguel Sotomayor/Moment; PeopleImages/E+; Eve Livesey/Moment; Kateryna Kon/Science Photo Library; LuzEnredada/Moment Open; Daniel Hernanz Ramos/Moment; Putra Kurniawan/EyeEm; Stocktrek Images; Zen Rial/Moment; Imgorthand/E+; Roland Magnusson/EyeEm; Phathn Sakdi Skul Phanthu/EyeEm; Wladimir Bulgar/Science Photo Library; Roc Canals Photography/Moment; FrankRamspott/DigitalVision Vectors; aristotoo/E+; Fertnig/E+; Fran Polito/Moment; Oleksandra Korobova/Moment; Fernando Trabanco Fotografía/Moment Open; Devon OpdenDries./Moment; druvo/E+; Blanchi Costela/Moment; mphillips007/E+; Miguel Sotomayor/Moment Open; Unggul Wicaksono/Moment; ThomasVogel/E+; Gallo Images - Martin Harvey/Riser/Getty Images Plus; Hero Images; Frank and Helena/Cultura; **U4:** amenic181/iStock/Getty Images Plus; Pablo_K/iStock/Getty Images Plus; Amarita/iStock/Getty Images Plus; lolostock/iStock/Getty Images Plus; R.Tsubin/Moment; lleerogers/iStock/Getty Images Plus; HandmadePictures/iStock/Getty Images Plus; smpics/iStock/Getty Images Plus; Spaces Images/Blend Images LLC; Pongsak Tawansaeng/EyeEm; Coprid/iStock/Getty Images Plus; sharrocks/iStock/Getty Images Plus; Avesun/iStock/Getty Images Plus; ValentynVolkov/iStock/Getty Images Plus; Hyrma/iStock/

Getty Images Plus; Instants/E+; Yaroslaw/iStock/Getty Images Plus; kurmyshov/iStock/Getty Images Plus; LauriPatterson/E+; Tetra images; Kerrick/iStock/Getty Images Plus; HelpingHandPhotos/iStock/Getty Images Plus; Foodcollection RF; Fancy Yan/Photodisc; gavran333/iStock/Getty Images Plus; Ulianna/iStock/Getty Images Plus; good_reason08/iStock/Getty Images Plus; carduus/DigitalVision Vectors; Lebazele/iStock/Getty Images Plus; Geber86/E+/Getty Images Plus; Erik Isakson; RubberBall Productions/Brand X Pictures; BlackJack3D/E+; Angelique Rademakers/EyeEm; Mike Kemp; Jose A. Bernat Bacete/Moment; HONG VO/iStock/Getty Images Plus; DanBrandenburg/E+; **U5:** .shock/iStock/Getty Images Plus; Tomas Jasinskis/EyeEm; Martin Blake/EyeEm; Michael Wheatley; Dzevoniia/iStock/Getty Images Plus; SimplyCreativePhotography/iStock/Getty Images Plus; Towfiqu Photography/Moment; DuncanL/iStock/Getty Images Plus; Boris SV/Moment; GIPhotoStock/Cultura; Carolyn Hebbard/Moment; Auscape/Universal Images Group/Getty Images Plus; Betsie Van der Meer/DigitalVision; PicturePartners/iStock/Getty Images Plus; Yatso/photo.com; Vladimiroquai/iStock/Getty Images Plus; Steve Lewis Stock/Photographer's Choice; Rhonda Gutenberg/Lonely Planet Images; Koldunova_Anna/iStock/Getty Images Plus; meteo021/iStock/Getty Images Plus; hipokrat/iStock/Getty Images Plus; artisteer/iStock/Getty Images Plus; amphotora/E+; Sandra Scheumann/EyeEm; Medioimages/Photodisc; Peter Dazeley/Photographer's Choice/Getty Images Plus; Luis Diaz Devesa/Moment; aga7ta/iStock/Getty Images Plus; Schon & Probst/Picture Press/Getty Images Plus; lleerogers/E+; Daniele Bonaldo/EyeEm; 4nadia/iStock/Getty Images Plus; RADsan/iStock/Getty Images Plus; Elizabeth Candy/EyeEm; belchonock/iStock/Getty Images Plus; artisteer/iStock/Getty Images Plus; SandroSalomon/iStock/Getty Images Plus; **U6:** ER Productions Limited/DigitalVision; studiocasper/iStock/Getty Images Plus; Bjorn Holland/Photographer's Choice RF; PhotoMelon/iStock/Getty Images Plus; Gary Conner/Photolibrary; farakos/iStock/Getty Images Plus; Philartphace/iStock/Getty Images Plus Unreleased; Tony Hutchings; Photographer's Choice; PhonlamaiPhoto/iStock/Getty Images Plus; Lebazele/iStock/Getty Images Plus; belchonock/iStock/Getty Images Plus; luchschen/iStock/Getty Images Plus; A_Pobedimskiy/iStock/Getty Images Plus; Wittayayut/iStock/Getty Images Plus; suriya silsaksom/iStock/Getty Images Plus; imagenavi; Image Source; Sjo/E+; alikemalkarasu/E+; Pauline St.Denis/Corbis/VCG/Corbis; pbombaert/Moment; ullstein bild; owattaphotos/iStock/GettyImages Plus; EireenZ/iStock/Getty Images Plus; sezgen/iStock/GettyImages Plus; Miguel ngel Carvajal Anaya/EyeEm; Martin Leigh/Oxford Scientific/Getty Images Plus; haryigit/iStock/Getty Images Plus; releon8211/iStock/Getty Images Plus; RASimon/iStock/Getty Images Plus; Martin Blake/EyeEm; Steve Debenport/E+; ourlifelooklikeballoon/iStock/Getty Images Plus; ARNICAart/iStock/Getty ImagesPlus; FrankRamspott/DigitalVision Vectors; GK Hart/Vikki Hart/Stockbyte; Avalon_Studio/E+; Morsa Images/Digital Vision; Rodolfo Parulan Jr./Moment; LokFung/DigitalVision Vectors.

The below mentioned photos are sourced from other library:
U0: Walter Oleksy/Alamy Stock Photo; **U4:** DonSmith/Alamy Stock Photo.

Front cover photography by Frank Greenaway/Dorling Kindersley/Getty Images plus/Getty Images; vnlit/iStock/Getty Images Plus/Getty Images; Josie Iselin/Visuals Unlimited, Inc./Getty Images; inhauscreative/iStock/Getty Images Plus/Getty Images; Víctor Del Pino/EyeEm/Getty Images; Don Mason/Corbis/Getty Images Plus/Getty Images; stilllifephotographer/Stone/Getty Images Plus/Getty Images; Dorling Kindersley: Gary Ombler/Getty Images Plus/Getty Images; David Curtis/EyeEm/Getty Images; Auscape/Universal Images Group/Getty Images; Geoff Dann/Dorling Kindersley/Getty Images Plus/Getty Images.

Designer: Chefer

The authors and publishers would like to thank the following illustrators:
Martyn Cain (Beehive Illustration) pp. 36–37, 40–41; Kay Coenen (Advocate Art) pp. 8 (t,b), 9–11, 12 (b), 13, 18, 19, 22, 24–27, 31, 46–48, 49 (l), 50, 52–53, 58, 60, 69 (c), 70 (c,b), 74, 79, 81; Sara Lynn Cramb (Astound US) p.72–73; Dave Smith (Beehive Illustration) pp. 7, 8 (cr), 12 (t), 14, 49 (r), 56–57, 62–63, 69 (t), 70 (t), 71 (t), 72–73, 85; Tom Woolley p. 72